D1266603

MODERN WITCHCRAFT
AND PSYCHOANALYSIS

Books by M. D. Faber

Suicide and Greek Tragedy

The Design Within: Psychoanalytic Approaches to Shakespeare
(Editor and Contributor)

*A New Anatomy of Melancholy: Patterns of Self-Aggression
Among Authors* (Co-Editor and Contributor)

*Culture and Consciousness: The Social Meaning of Altered
Awareness*

*Objectivity and Human Perception: Revisions and Crossroads
in Psychoanalysis and Philosophy*

*The Withdrawal of Human Projection: A Study of Culture and
Internalized Objects*

Modern Witchcraft and Psychoanalysis

MODERN WITCHCRAFT
AND PSYCHOANALYSIS

M. D. Faber

Rutherford • Madison • Teaneck
Fairleigh Dickinson University Press
London and Toronto: Associated University Presses

Associated University Presses
440 Forsgate Drive
Cranbury, NJ 08512

Associated University Presses
25 Sicilian Avenue
London WC1A 2QH, England

Associated University Presses
P.O. Box 338, Port Credit
Mississauga, Ontario,
Canada L5G 4L8

The paper used in this publication meets the requirements
of the American National Standard for Permanence of Paper
for Printed Library Materials Z39.48-1984.

Library of Congress Cataloging-in-Publication Data

Faber, M. D. (Mel D.)
    Modern witchcraft and psychoanalysis / M.D. Faber.
        p.   cm.
    Includes bibliographical references and index.
    ISBN 0-8386-3488-5 (alk. paper)
    1. Witchcraft. 2. Psychoanalysis. 3. Witchcraft—History.
4. Rites and ceremonies—Psychological aspects.   I. Title.
II. Title: Witchcraft and psychoanalysis.
BF1566.F27   1993
133.4'3'019—dc20   91-58949
                                                    CIP

For my children, Rebecca, Paul, and Ethan

Contents

Preface

About halfway through the writing of Chapter 3 I began to realize the extent to which I was dealing with what might be termed
archetypal materials. It occured to me that my analysis might
bear on religious ritual and symbolism, as well as on the occult,
in a broad sense. The cult of modern Witchcraft may eventually
outgrow its cultic status and develop into an alternative religion.
Conversely, it may in time shrink to a few scattered covens, or
even disappear. We don't know. But the symbols and the rites
that it employs will no doubt be around in one form or another
for a considerable period, just as they were around for a considerable period (some four or five thousand years) before modern
Witchcraft took them up. Thus, I would like to think that the
discussion to follow may foster psychoanalytic understanding
not only of Witchcraft particularly, but of religion and the occult
generally.

Psychoanalysis has always been intensely interested in group
behavior, although that interest has been overshadowed by its
concentration on the Oedipus complex, repression, infantile
sexuality, and the preoedipal, mother-infant relationship—in
short, the intrapsychic world of the individual and his/her significant other. Yet the fact that the first relationship, and indeed
all subsequent relationships, can only be grasped fully within a
social context, and that the social order, including, of course,
the family, is hugely determined by the tendencies of the individual as he emerges from the early period, should alert us to
the inextricable connection between group and individual psychology. Freud's *Group Psychology and the Analysis of the Ego*
and *Civilization and its Discontents* were among the first great
expressions of this theme and led, along with other influences
of course, to the writings of Herbert Marcuse, Norman O. Brown,
and Ernest Becker, and more recently to the work of Eli Sagan,
Howard Stein, and Richard Koenigsberg. I conceive of the present study as one that follows in this tradition, analyzing not
only religious (or cultic) symbols and behaviors but the group

dynamics involved in the coven and in the modern Witchcraft movement as a whole.

Obviously in my view psychoanalysis is a magnificent instrument with which to grasp both individual and group conduct. It gives us a particular, crucial kind of insight into what people are doing and what their actions *mean*. Because psychoanalysis is not an exact science, many regard it as unreliable and of little value as an investigative instrument. I will not venture into this hot and apparently endless debate here but only say to the reader that my analyses are supported by the clinical and theoretical edifice that psychoanalysis has built up over the years. While it is true that studying human beings, as opposed to, say, salt crystals, will always be a "soft" or inexact science, it is also true that the psychoanalytic net can catch a great deal in the way of underlying motivational significances. What all this boils down to, I suppose, is that the reader who is skeptical about— or hostile to—psychoanalysis may not discover as much in what follows as the reader who is open to it. As for the objection that the analytic approach places considerable emphasis on the early period of life, what can I say except that *is* psychoanalysis, that is how it views our existence. We are profoundly, ineluctably influenced in a thousand ways by the early stages of our development and by the internalizations which arise therefrom. With this, of course, I agree. My point is simply that to object that psychoanalysis has the tendency to spy aspects of the early period in life's later stages is like going to the opera and objecting that the characters on the stage are *singing*. It is the nature of the beast.

Chapter 1 offers the reader some historical and psychoanalyic background to the subsequent discussion. We look briefly at the work of Sir James Frazer, Margaret Murray, and Robert Graves, among others, in an effort to indicate the sources from which the trendsetters of the modern Witchcraft movement (Gerald Gardner, Margot Adler, Miriam Simos, or "Starhawk," et al.) take their inspiration. We then turn to the psychoanalytic writings of Freud, Roheim, Kluckhohn, and others to find out what psychoanalysis has had to say about Witches and Witchcraft to date.

Chapter 2 presents the model of human development that will serve as the foundation of the psychoanalysis which occurs in earnest in Chapters 3 and 4. In the main, the model is derived from the clinical and theoretical work of Margaret Mahler and her associates, and from recent advances in object relations theory. Here, we watch the human infant, child, and adolescent struggling with the problems of merger, separation, and differentiation. We explore the nature of infantile narcissism and its involvement in feelings of omnipotence and grandiosity, as well as in the dependent longing to fuse with the caretaker (usually the mother) and her substitutes. We begin to understand the extent to which individuals, throughout the course of the life cycle, strive to heal their narcissistic wounds by turning to activities and behaviors which restore their sense of merger with an omnipotent presence, along with their early sensations of security and bliss.

Chapter 3 is divided into two parts and forms the heart of the book. The first part explores in great detail the texts, rituals, and practices that comprise the core of modern Witchcraft. Because Miriam Simos's (or Starhawk's) *The Spiral Dance* figures so predominantly into the scene it begets a good deal of attention, along with the writings of Scott Cunningham, L. Warren-Clarke, Gerald Gardner, Margot Adler, and Janet and Stewart Farrar. Here we concentrate intensively on the magic circle, the notion of the four directions, the composition of the coven, the rites of initiation, the tools of Wicca such as the pentagram, the wand, the athame, the cords, and the cauldron, and on Wiccan rituals such as drawing down the moon, the circle of stones, the openings of the body, and the great rite (sexual intercourse). We also focus on such Wiccan (and occult) practices as astral travel, auric healing, channeling, and numerology. At every step of the way the presentation of the world of the Craft is tied closely to the previous chapter on human development so that the reader is able to perceive without interruption the psychoanalytic meaning of the objects and behaviors he is encountering. Part Two of this chapter presents the modern Witchcraft movement from the proverbial horse's mouth, that is, it consists of three interviews with members of the Craft (Natalie, Richard, and Mary), which allow the reader to "hear" firsthand why people gravitate to Wicca and how they understand its teaching and rites. There is no authorial, interpretative interruption of these materials. They are presented directly from tapes and notes, and they are designed to be read squarely in the light of the context. Here the psychoanalytic reader can judge for him/herself as to the meaning and purpose of this cult. Part Two concludes with an account of the author's attendance at a coven meeting during the spring of 1990. The reader is given a chance to see the Witches gathering in the home of the priestess, connecting themselves to the earth (grounding), and healing one of their fellow coveners through the magical transference of Wiccan power.

Chapter 4 comprises the book's conclusion and attempts to demonstrate the manner in which, and the degree to which, the absorptions in magic, omnipotence, and fusion that characterize the Craft find their way to other cultural activities in the areas of economics, politics, science, and technology. As we seek obsessively after wealth, as we devote ourselves fanatically to this or that ideology, as we pursue "the truth" through our scientific endeavors, as we strive to fashion with artificial intelligence a computer that is "conscious" or "fully alive" (cf. a recent edition of *Omni*), we may align ourselves motivationally and behaviorally with those who turn to the Goddess and her rituals in an effort to achieve immortality and power. This chapter asserts that what it calls "a ubiquity of bewitchment" is more than a facile analogy, that a variety of human pursuits are very close to Wicca in terms of their underlying (unconscious) significance. Modern Witchcraft, then, is not simply a cult of the so-called lunatic fringe. It springs up quite naturally in a culture that is given to a variety of narcissistic obsessions.

I wish to acknowledge my indebtedness to Colleen Donnelly of the English Department, University of Victoria. Ms. Donnelly's outstanding secretarial skills made the task much, much easier than it would otherwise have been.

MODERN WITCHCRAFT
AND PSYCHOANALYSIS

1

The Rise of the Witches and the Historical-Psychoanalytic Background

To read Margot Adler's (1986) definitive study of Neo-Paganism (of which the Craft, or Wicca, or Witchcraft is by far the most sizeable offshoot) is to come away with a variety of arresting facts: During the past three decades North America, Europe, and Australia have witnessed a "population explosion" within paganism, an "extraordinary proliferation of Witches' covens" that has culminated in the foundation of the Witches' International Craft Association with headquarters in New York. The Wiccan Church of Canada with headquarters in Toronto, Wicca Française with headquarters in Paris, and, finally, to round out the picture, the Pagan Anti-Defamation League with headquarters in London. This last group is dedicated to correcting misconceptions about "Wicca," the "natural faith of Britain" (51, 455, 529).

According to Adler, there are approximately one hundred thousands active, self-identified pagans or members of Wicca in the United States alone, and many thousands more (both in and out of the closet) throughout the world. What Adler calls "the Wichcraft movement" is experiencing more and more acceptance in the larger culture. Books on "the Goddess" have entered the mainstream of religious and philosophic thought. Serious scholarship is taking place both inside and outside the universities. There is less persecution. There are more children in Wiccan communities, and more attention is being paid to their needs. More older people are getting involved, as well as more highly skilled people including computer programmers, doctors, lawyers, architects, anthropologists, accountants, welders, machinists, nurses, market analysts, and scientists. One can easily come away from Adler's book believing that Witches are taking over the world. That is, of course, a long way from the truth; but "the movement" has unquestionably achieved a certain influence, and the future will probably see that influence increase. Witchcraft may still be a cult, but it is rapidly becoming a prominent one whose cultic status could be outgrown by the end of the century.

I approach the rebirth of Witchcraft from a psychoanalytic perspective with several major purposes in view. First, I want to discover what Witchcraft *means* to the individuals who are getting involved. I want to explore the emotions, the wishes, the fantasies of these people and by doing so, shed light not only upon the deep, underlying reasons for participation in this particular cultic and religious movement but hopefully upon the reasons for participation in cultic and religious movements generally. I am interested in Witchcraft as a *representative example* of the way in which religions and cults attract people for powerful emotional reasons that are rooted in the dynamic unconscious, the facet of the human mind which is tied inextricably to the formative years and to the compelling parental presences therein.

Let me hasten to say, however, that I do not mean to discount conscious, or what psychoanalysis calls secondary, factors. On the contrary, I hope to demonstrate how the individual's current, conscious concerns motivate and drive him, how his social, political, economic, and interpersonal preoccupations influence his choices. There will be no wholesale reduction here. At the same time, to stress my main interest again, there will be no discounting of the unconscious dimension, no easy, comfortable setting aside of the subsurface forces that typically constrain one's conduct, especially where religions and cults are concerned. Hopefully, in the end, we will see how unconscious fantasy and wish combine with conscious considerations to produce the individual's behavior.

Second, and this point has already been anticipated in the previous paragraph, I am interested in exploring the Craft analytically with an eye to disclosing its meaning *in* and *to* the culture within which it operates. I do not believe we can say clearly what the movement means to the individual without placing him in a social context and without examining his relationship to the social world that surrounds him. What we must always bear in mind, however, is the fully two-sided nature of this relationship. The social order both impinges on the individual and is impinged on by him. Indeed, the objects that make up the person's inner world, the parental presences deeply embedded in his unconscious, are characteristically *projected into* the cultural realm which becomes, in turn, an expression or "symbol" of the parent-as-perceived-by-the-offspring. The power of social institutions, such as Witchcraft, is largely derived from the power of the first relationship with the parental figures. Norman O. Brown (1959, 154) puts the matter succinctly when he writes that "human culture exists in order to project the infantile conflicts into concrete reality where they can be seen and mastered." In this way, my social analyses are designed to complement, or complete, my analyses of individual wishes and needs.

I want also to examine involvement in the Craft as a way for the individual to express his explicitly *moral* concerns, his sensitivity to the ethical issues that swirl around him in the social order. During the past half century Witchcraft has become more and more absorbed with problems such as the environment, nuclear weapons, the rights of women, gays, and other minorities, animal experimentation, and religious freedom. As it turns out, psychoanalysis during the past half century has undergone a reevaluation of its moral theories, gravitating away from the primacy of the paternal superego and toward the importance of the nurturance and care that are internalized into the person's moral center as he interacts with the maternal figure. In Wiccan terms, the moral theories of psychoanalysis are disclosing a tendency to put the Goddess in the place of the God. Thus, to probe the morality of Witchcraft will give us a chance to appreciate not only the relationship between theological beliefs and moral conduct, but the advance in moral understanding that the new psychoanalysis has engendered.

Implicit in the shift from God to Goddess is the need to study Withcraft in relation to *both* sexes, to distinguish carefully the significance of its teachings for the men who get involved and for the women who get involved. Largely because of Freud's well-known reluctance to look squarely at the preoedipal period, not to mention his patriarchal leanings, psychoanalysis struggled unsuccessfully for many years to develop an adequate theory of female as opposed to male development. Indeed, at one point in his career, Freud came to the astonishing conclusion that the male's development was the normative one and the female's a failed version of it, rooted in her envy of the penis. For Freud, this explained the female's preponderant emotionalism, her inability to develop the powers of reason, judgment, morality—all of which were more characteristic of men. By the 1970s Freud's ideas had been corrected through the writings of Melanie Klein,

D. W. Winnicott, Margaret Mahler, Robert Stoller, and others, who gave us a full, rich account of woman's unique development, a psychologically sensitive grasp of what it means to be a woman. Accordingly, psychoanalysis has of late become an ally of the women's movement. As is so often the case, a mistake on the part of a great man eventually pays off in greater understanding. It is precisely this greater understanding that I mean to apply to the Craft. Witches and Warlocks are to be distinguished not only in terms of their anatomy, but also in terms of the developmental needs they bring to the Wiccan community.

As we peruse Margot Adler's list of adherents to the movement and as we take note of the scientists, lawyers, doctors, skilled tradesmen, and teachers who have become involved, we realize that the old dichotomy of reason versus passion, or rationality versus irrationality, will not be very useful in working up a psychoanalysis of Witchcraft. We cannot pass off the rise of the Witches as simply an outbreak of unreason in a reasonable age, a collective psychosis, or an expression of the "lunatic fringe." It just is not that sort of movement. It is made up of more or less ordinary folk, the kind one finds working in hospitals, hotels, machine shops, and corner stores; it is a society that is loaded with "normal, average people," with those who are no more "neurotic" than many of the individuals who regularly attend synagogue on Saturday or church on Sunday. This is not, of course, a legitimation or justification of anything, but it is an indication that a facile employment of the notion of aberrancy will not get us very far. Indeed, Witchcraft today has for many people become merely an alternative religion, an alternative way of expressing spiritual aspirations, of participating in a transcendent realm of divine mysteries and forces, all of which we associate with religion in the usual sense.

Far from comprising an impediment to our study, this actually allows us to grasp more fully the unconscious agenda that inheres not only in all religion but in all those human pursuits which elicit strong, emotional participation. Which brings me to my final purpose: I plan to use my study of the Craft to develop analytic understanding of the way we approach a variety of key, cultural activities such as economics, politics, and science. Odd as it may appear at first glance, I plan to disclose what these cultural spheres may have in common with Witchcraft. In addition, I will offer suggestions, rooted firmly in psychoanalysis, as to how we might alter our characteristic participation in culture in ways that might improve our situation on the planet. In a nutshell, I will use my study of Witchcraft to speculate on what might be called the evolution of human behavior in the cultural realm. The wonderful thing about Wicca, its religious and perceptual assumptions, its absorption in magic, its preoccupation with power, and its quest for personal efficacy in an age of gigantic, impersonal forces, is that it raises all the big issues, the ones that oblige us to consider afresh just what sort of creature we are.

Some Historical and Psychoanalytic Background: The Bad Witch

Psychoanalytic studies of Witchcraft to date focus on four major topics: the nature and persistence of ancient religions, the persecutions in Europe and America during the sixteenth and seventeenth centuries, the meaning of Witchcraft among native peoples such as the Navaho and the Normanby Islanders, and the significance of the Witch in the popular fairy tale. As we shall see, explorations of these areas are extremely helpful in understanding the nature and meaning of Witchcraft today.

As one might expect, the current revival of the Craft derives from a great many sources. Among the most important of these is the historical work on ancient European and Near-Eastern religions that commenced toward the turn of the last century with Sir James Frazer's *The Golden Bough* (1890) and that continued into the twentieth century with Margaret A. Murray's *The Witch-Cult in Western Europe* (1921), and Robert Graves's *The White Goddess* (1946). I will move briskly through these rich, complex materials, and through a variety of comments upon them, in an effort to draw forth the key, psychoanalytic implications.

Frazer's *Golden Bough* depicts several ancient fertility cults—each of which was based on the figure of a god who dies and is reborn, and whose death and rebirth are associated with the cycle of the seasons, or the harvesting and sowing of the crops. According to Norman Cohn (1975, 107), whose seminal work *Europe's Inner Demons* we will examine shortly, Frazer's study launched a "cult of fertility cults" during the first two decades of the twentieth century, and it is precisely these cults that we may regard as the foundation of the modern Witchcraft movement.

Graves maintained in *The White Goddess,* "perhaps the book

which has had the greatest effect on modern Wicca" (Cunningham 1988, 206), that the ancient religions depicted by Frazer were originally goddess, not god, centered. The gods came later as male or "patriarchal" forces and overwhelmed the original mother-centered institutions in a quest for power—the effects of which we are still feeling today. In this, Graves was following earlier theorists such as Engles and Bachofen whose work, he believed, had been largely and erroneously ignored as a result of Frazer's popularity. Graves's study was (and is) particularly appealing to those who believe a return to goddess worship can lead human beings toward a more benign, nurturant treatment of the planet and each other than that which has been obtained during the rapacious, aggressive patriarchal era. A dramatic rise in goddess-centered covens during the 1940s and 1950s is traditionally attributed to Graves's work, although goddess worship was well underway by then.

It was well underway largely because of Margaret Murray's *Witch-Cult in Western Europe.* A folklorist, anthropologist, and Egyptologist, Murray examined the works of Bachofen, Engles, Frazer, and most importantly, the trial documents of the Catholic Inquisition. She concluded not only that Witchcraft could be traced to pre-Christian times but that it constituted the ancient religion of Western Europe. A fertility cult in the tradition of Frazer's *Golden Bough,* this "organized religion" had originated among an aboriginal British race of "small people" who subsequently gave rise to the belief in fairies, as reflected, for example, in Shakespeare's *A Midsummer Night's Dream.* Meeting *en masse* at eight major festivals, or sabbats, and at smaller gatherings, or esbats, in covens of thirteen, the Witches practiced an exuberant religion. They danced, feasted, and underwent visionary, shamanistic experiences. When the trial reports of the Inquisition accused Witches of flying through the air and changing themselves into animals, they were simply mistaking ritualistic for actual events. Indeed, the Witch was giving "a clear account of ... herself and her companions believing in the change of form caused by [a] magical object in exactly the same way that the shamans believe in their own transformation by similar means." Thus the Inquisition transformed the Witches' god into the devil, and replaced good with evil. However, it was also Murray's view that the coven, the sabbat, and various other facets of Witchcraft described in the trial reports were grounded in reality (1921, 12, 233, 236).

For three decades Murray's theory prevailed, sparking a rise of covens that was, as indicated, given significant, additional impetus by Graves's *White Goddess.* But as scholars began to investigate the theory they spied a variety of problems which eventually rendered it untenable. Professionals who still believe in it are no longer to be found, although Murray, who lived to be one hundred, refused to retract a single syllable in spite of the mounting criticism. What were the chief difficulties? First, Murray regarded as authentic accounts of witchery that were fabricated under torture; second, she offered evidence of pagan survivals in Britain but no evidence of any organized religion, or even of any widespread pagan remnants; and finally, she provided no evidence at all for the existence of covens or sabbats before the trial reports were penned.

These difficulties led to three main explanations, the last of which is psychoanalytic and central to our discussion as a whole.

According to Professor Trevor-Roper (1970), the Witch-craze of Europe and America that transpired during the sixteenth and seventeenth centuries was a product of the Inquisition, provoked deliberately to weed out heretics and to control religious views. True, pagan folk beliefs and magical practices existed during the Dark Ages, and what came to be called Witchcraft did include elements of pagan belief, but one must not "confuse the scattered fragments of paganism with the grotesque system into which they are only long afterward arranged." It was when the Church took the old beliefs and fashioned a demonology, including the sabbat, the coven, and most of all, the pact with the devil, that the scattered remnants of paganism became an organized system.

At first, contends Trevor-Roper, the Church employed the system against recalcitrant factions close to home, where it might have disappeared; but with the onset of the Reformation, the Church "revived the dying Witch-craze just as it had revived so many other obsolescent habits of thought: biblical fundamentalism, theological history, scholastic Aristotelianism." With the intensification of the "ideological war" and the "accompanying climate of fear," the Witch-craze acquired a "momentum of its own," eventually becoming part of the social fabric, as witnessed by similarities in the confessions at trial. The best minds of the day believed in the "new mythology," which faded away only as society underwent fundamental change (121–46).

For Mircea Eliade (1976), the pagan beliefs and magical practices of medieval Europe were more systematic than Trevor-Roper indicates and less systematic than Margaret Murray contends. Many of the features associated with European Witches (flying through the air, killing at a distance, mastering demons) may be found in other cultures such as India and Tibet; they may also be found in European countries such as Romania where there was no systematic maltreatment of Witches. In this way, "Witchcraft cannot be the creation of religious or political persecution." While there is no evidence for Murray's organized system of covens, there is plenty of documentary proof for the existence of groups such as the *benandanti* of Italy who fought ritualistic battles with wizards *(stregoni)* and who practiced fertility rites derived from the distant past. Witchcraft has timeless, universal features, as well as features arising from a particular culture and from a particular social situation (71).

Eliade's postulation of universal practices and beliefs leads directly to Norman Cohn's psychoanalytic theory set forth in his book, *Europe's Inner Demons* (1975). The figure of the Witch, says Cohn, derives largely from a specific, ancient fantasy: In the midst of the social order there exists a tiny, secret society hostile to the majority and engaged in a variety of inhuman practices including infanticide, cannibalism (particularly the eating of babies), orgiastic, bestial sexuality, and incest. One discover this fantasy among the Romans of the second century who used it to persecute the Christians, and one finds it later among the Christians who used it to persecute the Jews as well as heretical sects such as the Cathars and Knights Templars. For the peasants of Europe, Witches were simply those individuals, mostly old women, "who could bring down misfortune by a glance or a curse." But for the "bishops and inquisitors, . . . a Witch was above all a member of a secret, conspiratorial body organized and headed by Satan. Such a Witch could as well be a man as a woman, and just as well young as old" (252). The point is, "the notion of a secret society of Witches cannot be satisfactorily explained by postulating the real existence of such a society." Indeed, the "tradition" that such a society exists "forms a curious chapter in the history of ideas" and may be attributed ultimately to "grossly underestimating the capacities of human imagination" (125). It is the "demonological obsessions" of Europe that stand behind both the notion of the evil, clandestine sect and the stereotype of the Witch who customarily functions therein.

The questions arise, to what may we attribute the origin of this obsessional fantasy that comes down to us through the centuries more or less unchanged, and how does the figure of the Witch relate specifically to that origin? Reminding us that what he has been examining is "above all a fantasy at work in history," Cohn states that the nature of Europe's inner demons is indicated "by the specific accusations brought against the demonized groups," namely, cannibalistic infanticide and orgiastic, incestuous sexuality. In regard to the former, "psychoanalysts maintain that its unconscious roots lie in infancy or early childhood." More specifically, "the infant in the first two years of life experiences cannibalistic impulses which he projects onto his parents." Other psychoanalysts, notes Cohn, "suggest that many parents really do harbor unconscious cannibalistic impulses towards their children, and that the children are subliminally aware of the fact." In this way, the theme of cannibalistic infanticide and the stereotype of the Witch that frequently accompanies it (as in the documents of the Inquisition or in the story of Hansel and Gretel) "owe part of their appeal to wishes and anxieties experienced in infancy or early childhood." In regard to the theme of orgiastic sexuality and incest, "it is a simple matter to interpret." It "does not refer to real happenings but reflects repressed desires, or if one prefers, feared temptations." It is "certainly" the product of "unconscious projections" fostered in part by a Christian order that has "tended to exalt spiritual values at the expense of the animal side of human nature" (261–62). Such are the psychoanalytic essentials of *Europe's Inner Demons.*

It would be difficult in this limited space to do justice to Cohn's overall thesis. He marshalls forth an enormous amount of skillfully organized evidence in support of his ideas which are, in my view at least, very convincing. But what is particularly important here is the way Cohn's book guides us toward three key points that we may keep in mind for the remainder of this study. First, Witchcraft, in the broadest sense, including the figure of the Witch and all the magical practices involved in the Craft, is inextricably, powerfully, and unconsciously bound up with the early period of human life, the period during which the infant and small child interact physically and emotionally with the parents, and in particular with the mother. Second, the behaviors of Witches and Warlocks (as perceived by others or as really occurring) are characteristically projective, fantasy versions of specific emotional and physical events that transpired in the individual's actual past. Witchcraft makes sense from a number of perspectives, and one of these is the developmental history of the doer/perceiver. Third, Witchcraft is a way of dealing with repressed desires. Cohn lays the emphasis on repressed sexuality, and he does so because his historical materials require it. As we shall see, however, the psychodynamics of Witchcraft involve a variety of aims including, most notably, those that spring from the urge to omnipotently extend one's ego boundaries out into the external world, far beyond the realm of the limited self.

Freud would have agreed with many of Cohn's points. Although he never wrote systematically about Witchcraft, he did purchase books on the subject, including the notorious *Malleus Maleficarum,* the official description of the Witch cult written during the inquisition by two Dominican friars. Thinking about Witches in a letter to Fliess, he makes the observation that a person who is being tortured, or who is suffering from mental illness, is apt to confess to all sorts of things, including a pact with the devil (Freud 1985, 97, 224–25). In another letter, he remarks ironically that many of the tales his patients tell about the evil influence of their families and friends call to mind the accusations customarily brought against Witches. He then proceeds to declare that the Witch hunts of Europe were rooted in widespread, collective paranoia, and in the tendency to attribute to others inclinations lurking unconsciously in oneself. This is, of course, very close to Cohn, although Freud lays no emphasis here on the significance of early infancy and childhood (Freud 1985, 227). As for Cohn's emphasis on repressed sexuality and all the madness *that* engenders, it would be very difficult indeed to imagine Freud disagreeing.

Anthropological Perspectives: The Bad Witch Continued

Further support for Cohn's view, and for the widening of it that I am beginning to develop here, may be discovered in anthropological studies undertaken from a psychoanalytic perspective. Roheim, working with the Normanby Islanders of the Australian Pacific, directs our attention to an ancient tale called *Our Mothers:*

> In old times when the mothers of our own mothers lived, there were two Witches. One of them was called Butumaija (Our fame) and the other Bomutu (Rub it on the end). The first Witch used to call to the second one: "Bomutu, there is a boat." "You wreck it, I can't because I have to hold my child." The Witches capsize the boats in order to eat the voyagers. (Roheim 1950, 157)

"The two Witches," observes Roheim, "are really the one Witch-Mother." The Witch who capsizes the boat "is the one who holds (rocks) the child." Yet, Roheim continues, "the Witches eat the voyagers they have wrecked; that is, if we remember that the two Witches are really the same Witch, this means that the mother who frustrates the child becomes the cannibal Witch." Maintaining that the frustration of the nursing infant is among life's earliest and most profound traumas, Roheim concludes that "the Witch is the typical talio representative of the child's body destruction fantasy—the bad mother" (179). We have here, needless to say, another reminder of Cohn's thesis as we expanded it a few paragraphs earlier: The origins of the Witch and of the rites she practices are to be found in the early period and particularly in the child's powerful, projective fantasies concerning the mother who threatens, frustrates, and disappoints.

Nor does Cohn's emphasis on sexual factors go unsupported in Roheim who, after examining more Normanby tales, observes that a Witch may mean "sexual desire" and the feeling of "guilt" that normally accompanies both incest and sexual interaction with an alluring parental substitute. "The trend *toward the mother*," Roheim writes in a major utterance, "is the basic element in the trend *away from the mother*" (198). The Normanby Islanders are "running away from the mother and they are trying to find a new mother." But "the mother of the past, or rather their own oral aggression, pursues them in the shape of the cannibal Witch." Translated into psychological language this means, "our mothers won't let us grow up" (199). And then, "substitute objects are found, yet the substitute is in a sense really the same as the original; and all this is achieved with plenty of anxiety" (201). Thus "the Witch's way is the mother's way, and the [Sorcerer's] way is the father's way" (201). In the "eyes of a male," the Witch is "really his mother," and his conception of her "revolves" around the "theme" of "oral frustration."

But Roheim also makes clear that oral frustration is finally apprehended by the child as a form of rejection, negation, *separation,* not merely the interrruption of a feed. The ultimate anxiety is the anxiety of parental *loss:*

There was a little boy who had a *gatura* (a kind of fish). *His mother and father took the fish and ate it.* So he cried from morning to evening. They grew very tired of this. After having cooked two pots of food for him they loaded their canoe with taro, yams, and bananas and *left while the child was still asleep.* They went away, and the

Witch came out; that is, the parents who leave *are* the bad mother. (216)

Summing up in the light of this passage, Roheim declares, "the infant in general (not only on Normanby Island) starts life in the psychological situation of unity with the mother, and from this unity it disidentifies itself through the frustrations it inevitably suffers and through the aggressions called forth by those frustrations" (217). Thus does Roheim assist our expansion of the psychological picture found in Cohn: Witchcraft is associated not only with the early period, with projection, the bad object, and the repression of sexual aims; it is integrally connected to ambivalent feelings in the area of separation and growth. The child, on the one hand, fears separation; he wants to stay with the mother, to preserve the original union. On the other hand, the child wants and needs to separate, to escape the stunting of his psychological growth that prolonged union with the mother would bring. This is the key issue, and often the most tormenting issue, of life's first years; it underlies the themes of oral aggression and forbidden sexuality, and it is directly connected to the figure of the Witch at the level of unconscious process.

Working with the Navaho of the American Southwest, Kluckhohn (1982) observes that the existence of Witchcraft as an institution serves several purposes. It gives mediocre people of low social standing a chance to move to the center of the stage and, as Witches, to appear interesting and mysterious. It also allows every member of the society to indulge his forbidden aggressive and sexual fantasies without inordinate guilt—he can blame them on the Witches, and it allows the conformist majority to bring rebels and troublemakers back into line by accusing them of trafficking with demons. Of particular importance for us here, however, is not only Kluckhohn's contention that "early life" provides the foundation for the Navaho belief in Witches, but that early life *as it is tied specifically to the issue of parental omnipotence* harbors crucial meaning:

> The child, even before he is fully responsive to verbalizations, begins to get a picture of experience as potentially menacing. He sees his parents, and other elders, confess their impotence to deal with various matters in that they resort to prayers, songs, and magical observances. When he has been linguistically socialized he hears the hushed gossip of Witchcraft. . . . The mother, who has been seen not only as a prime source of gratification but also as an almost omnipo-

tent person, is now revealed as herself afraid, at the mercy of threatening forces. (247)

Navaho children are frequently ill, frequently hungry, and often
confused by the partial adoption of American and European
"dietary habits" and "other borrowings" (248). In this way, "a
belief in Witches fits with what the young Navaho very soon
comes to expect of living." Witchcraft becomes "a potential avenue to supernatural power," to regaining the sense of omnipotence felt in the early relationship with the mothering figure.
The "practices of Witchcraft" are "regressive instruments" employed by persons who "lust for power," who are "on the spot"
and less able to "take it" than others (249, 259).

The tie between the Navaho search for omnipotence (or "lust
for power") and a similar questing among the members of the
modern Witch-cult has yet to be established, of course. Yet if I
may be permitted to add the implications of Kluckhohn's study
to the generalized picture I am developing here, I would suggest,
first, that separation from the mother impinges anxiously upon
the infant not merely as it forces him to confront his isolation
but also as it forces him to confront the loss of his magical
efficacy, and second, that Witchcraft everywhere, in all locations
and cultures, is rooted partly in the effort to undo and deny that
loss.

The materials we have examined thus far attest to a splitting
of the maternal presence in the psychological origins of Witchcraft. The figure of the Witch is integrally bound up with the
emergence of what psychoanalysis calls the "bad object" during
the first months and years of life. Yet those months and years
are as crucially linked to the "good object" as they are to the
"bad." Moreover, our experience tells us that good Witches also
play a role (although a considerably smaller one than that played
by bad Witches) in the overall cultural and historical picture.
Accordingly, I will round out this Introduction by offering a word
or two on the good side of the split, and on the meaning of good
associations in the psychological origins of the Craft.

The Good Object in Hansel and Gretel

Bruno Bettelheim (1976) gets at the essence of the matter in
his classic study, *The Uses of Enchantment*. What we must bear
in mind here is the way the Good Witch usually appears in close

association to, and often in close proximity with, the Bad Witch. From a psychoanalytic perspective, this speaks for the ubiquity of ambivalent motivations during the first years of life, and in particular during the period in which the child is struggling to maintain his connection to the mother at the same time that he is struggling to get some distance from her.

Reminding us that the Witch is above all "the creation of our wishes and anxieties," Bettelheim asks, "who would not like to have the power of the Witch, and use it to satisfy all his desires, and to punish his enemies?" (94). More than the other creations of our imagination that we invest with magical power, he goes on to relate that the Witch, "in her opposite aspects," is a "reincarnation of the all-good mother and all bad-mother" of infancy and early childhood. It is precisely these two aspects of the Witch that are delineated in numerous fairy tales. "In these stories (*Hansel and Gretel, The Two Brothers, The Goose Girl*), the Witch resembles the way in which the pre-oedipal mother appears to the child: all-giving, all-satisfying, as long as he does not insist on doing things his way and remains symbiotically tied to her." However, says Bettelheim, "as the child begins to assert himself and do more on his own, the 'No's' naturally increase," and the child begins to experience a "deep disenchantment: What has given him bread has turned to stone" (95). The point is, "whatever the age of a person, when he is confronted with the problem of whether to break away from his parents, there is always a wish to have an existence entirely free of them, along with the opposite desire to remain bound closely to them," for there is "no greater threat in life than that we will be deserted, left all alone. Psychoanalysis has named this— man's greatest fear—separation anxiety" (95, 147). We have here, of course, a striking corroboration of Roheim's points that oral frustration is ultimately linked to separation anxiety and that the figure of the Witch is a projective verson of the parent who abandons or appears to abandon the child.

Turning to *Hansel and Gretel,* Bettelheim reminds us that the children believe their parents are plotting to desert them. "A small child awakening hungry in the darkness of the night," he writes, "feels threatened by complete rejection and desertion, which he experiences in the form of starvation" (159). Because the mother represents the source of all food to the children, it is she who is now experienced as abandoning them, "as if in a wilderness." It is the child's "anxiety and deep disappointment when Mother is no longer willing to meet all his oral demands" that leads him to believe Mother has become "unloving, selfish, rejecting." After being deserted for the first time, Hansel and Gretel attempt to return home simply because they know they need their parents, but this solves nothing. Indeed, by implication, the story is revealing here the "debilitating consequences of trying to deal with life's problems by means of regression and denial": During the second desertion Hansel foolishly attempts to mark the path home with bread crumbs which the birds quickly devour. "Bread stands here for food in general, man's 'life line,' an image which Hansel takes literally, out of his anxiety." This discloses the "limiting effects of fixations to primitive levels of development," resorted to "out of fear" (159).

In amplifying his thesis, Bettelheim points out that *Hansel and Gretel* expresses the "anxieties and learning tasks of the young child who must overcome and sublimate his primitive incorporative and hence destructive desires." He must learn "that if he does not free himself of these, his parents or society will force him to do so against his will." In this tale, however, it is the "mothering figure" who is "linked directly" to the crucial "inner experiences." The father "remains a shadowy and ineffectual figure throughout." Frustrated, hungry, and abandoned, Hansel and Gretel "give full rein to their oral regression" as they confront the gingerbread house. They "think nothing of destroying what should give shelter and safety." Symbolically, this house, which one can "eat up," stands for the "good mother" who offers her body as a source of nourishment. It is "the original all-giving mother, whom every child hopes to find again later somewhere out in the world, when his own mother begins to impose restrictions."

But as the story reveals, such "unrestrained giving in to gluttony" threatens destruction; regression to the earliest state of bliss "does away with all individuation." It even "endangers one's very existence as cannibalistic inclinations are given body in the figure of the Witch" (161). A personification of destructive orality, she wants to eat the children as much as they want to eat the house, and it is her "evil design" that finally obliges Hansel and Gretel to "recognize the dangers of unrestrained oral greed and dependence." As they do this, the "way to a higher stage of development opens up." More specifically—and we reach here the heart of the discussion—they discover that the "good, giving mother was hidden deep down in the bad, destructive one because there are treasures to be gained: the children inherit the Witch's jewels, which become valuable to them after they return

home—that is, after they can again find the good parent." For
Bettelheim, this suggests that as the children "transcend their
oral anxiety" and free themselves from relying on "oral satisfaction for security"; they can also "free themselves of the image of
the threatening mother—the Witch—and rediscover the good
parents, whose greater wisdom—the shared jewels—then benefits all" (162). Thus Hansel and Gretel become "more mature
children", they find their way "toward a higher plane of psychological and intellectual existence." What has changed at the end
of the tale is mainly "inner attitudes." No more will the children
"feel pushed out"; nor will they seek the gingerbread house. "But
neither will they encounter or fear the Witch" whom they have
"outsmarted." Bettelheim concludes, "as long as children continue to believe in Witches—they always have and always will,
up to the age when they no longer are compelled to give their
formless apprehensions humanlike appearance—they need to
be told stories in which children, by being ingenious, rid themselves of these persecuting figures of their imagination" (166).

Bettelheim's probing interpretation, on the one hand, underscores virtually everything that we have said about Witchcraft
and the figure of the Witch thus far: Both are bound up dynami-
cally with the anxieties and wishes of the early period, with
feelings of ambivalence in the area of separation and growth, and
with the tendency to externalize or project one's inner world, in
this case through the metaphors of gingerbread and jewels, and
through the split version of the maternal object. On the other
hand, Bettelheim's study opens up what we can call an adaptive
or evolutionary perspective. It reminds us that there are a *variety* of ways to deal with the anxiety and ambivalence of the early
time. In relation primarily to the figure of the Bad Witch, one
can simply project one's fears into other people or creatures or
things, creating and "finding" monsters and victims in the external world; when other people are involved, this is usually called
scapegoating. One can regress to the early stages of parent-child
interaction, seeking the original home, the womb, the garden,
the perfect bliss of eternal symbiosis, the endless, uninterrupted feed, or one can seek to recapture the first, magical relationship through one's questing for omnipotence, unlimited
power over the environment, or the attainment of a godlike stat-
ure. As Bettelheim asked, "Who would not have the power of the
Witch?" This reminds us, of course, that the Witch-persecutors
in Cohn, the paranoid patients in Freud, the makers of Witch
stories in Roheim, and the power-seeking Witches in Kluckhohn

are not simply sadistic or superstitious or sick individuals. Without minimizing their responsibility and pathology for even one moment, we can see that such people are trying to deal with their deepest, inward anxieties and conflicts, the legacies of their own unique infancies and childhoods.

By contrast, and in relation to the figure of the Good Witch (or good object), one can endeavor to *work through* his primal anxieties and fears, his backward, regressive inclinations, his urge to project into others his own unresolved ambivalence and anger, and by doing this, one can achieve a higher level of functioning, a resolution of impossible, conflicting aims, and a measure of integration and harmony. In a word, one can *use* the "bad," the regressive, the projective to forge a new path toward growth. The wisdom and strength inherent in the good side of the split can, through a transformative process, be made one's own.

When we take all this together, that is, when we concentrate on *both* sides of the split, we discover the key questions that we will ask of Witchcraft today: To what extent do our Witches succeed in becoming big Hansels and big Gretels? Alternatively, to what extent does the Craft bespeak a genuine effort to work through and resolve the basic problems of separation and growth that we have touched on in the context? To what extent does the Craft bespeak a refusal to relinquish infantile wishes and demands, a regressive striving for omnipotence and merger—in short, a denial of reality? To put the issue in the key terms that we discovered in Roheim, to what extent is Witchcraft today a movement back toward the original object of symbiotic union, and to what extent is a movement away from the object toward maturity and integration? To determine this, *precisely this,* will constitute our psychoanalysis of Witchcraft.

However, because our psychoanalysis will be hugely dependent on our expert understanding of human development, particularly as it transpires during the first years of life, and because this Introduction merely touched on that topic in a passing way, we must take a few pages to go more fully and more deeply into it. When we get to the Witches, as we will shortly do, we want to be very sharp, very incisive indeed, in our ability to see exactly what they are at, and exactly what their attitudes, beliefs, and ritualistic behaviors mean.

2

Merger, Separation, and Omnipotence:
On the Way to Wicca

A New Province of Knowledge

In the next few pages, I will describe a revolution in human understanding. This revolution has been going on for about one hundred years; it harbors an enormous potential for improving human relations, indeed, human existence generally; it has catalyzed and continues to catalyze major changes in our private and public conduct both as children and adults; and finally, it allows us to discern the motivational dynamics not only of Witchcraft as we know it today but of a great many other institutions and movements throughout the world. I am referring to the comprehensive study of human infancy and childhood.

Until recently, babies were routinely operated upon without anesthetics because the doctors believed the babies did not feel pain. Astounding as that may seem it is not untypical of the ignorance and insensitivity that Westerners have displayed toward infants over the centuries. If the reader has an appetite for this horror story, I refer him to the work of those psycho-historians who have been devoting themselves to the subject for about thirty years (cf. de Mause 1982). Although the mistreatment of babies is still a common occurrence, and may always be common given the tendency of people to transfer their frustrations and discontentments to their offspring, we are at last beginning to grasp in some depth what might be called the nature of the infant's special world.

It will be my contention in this chapter, as it is my contention in this book, that we cannot grasp the nature of social institutions apart from this new and revolutionary knowledge. Unless we are willing to view social institutions as addressing, or attempting to resolve, the dilemmas of infancy and childhood, we will simply miss out. Our understanding will not merely be partial; it will be hopelessly flawed, hopelessly incomplete. That is the nature of genuine revolutions: they change perceptions, and they leave behind those who are unable or unwilling to have their perceptions changed.

Psychoanalysis was instrumentally bound up, of course, with the advent of this revolution, and because psychoanalysis was a new discipline with huge and difficult territories to chart, and many original minds were involved in the charting, the revolution went forward amidst considerable controversy. Although Freud made important contributions to the understanding of infantile sexuality and narcissism, his own personal resistance to the study of the mother-infant bond, as well as his preoccupation with the Oedipus complex (the second resulted in some measure from the first), discouraged investigators from examining meticulously the psychological realities of the early period. However, by the 1930s through the pioneering work of Melanie Klein and her followers, and by the 1950s through the work of Winnicott, Fairbairn, and Spitz, significant and permanent inroads were being made into this new province of knowledge. People were beginning to appreciate in earnest the degree to which the mind and the emotions are shaped, even determined, by the original relationship between the parent and the child.

I am not suggesting that controversy ceased after Freud's resistances were skirted. There was still disagreement, and there will always be disagreement given the problematical nature of the subject and the difficulty of devising so-called objective measures. Does the relation between mother and infant govern the nature and growth of the instinctual endowment? Can what psychoanalyis calls "instinct theory" be reconciled with what it calls "object relations theory"? *Are* there instincts at all in any true sense of the word? What is the father's role during the formative years? And what about changing patterns of infant care? Such questions are raised routinely in a variety of psychoanalytic publications; obviously, we are not going to resolve them here once and for all. What we can underscore, however, is that by the present day a remarkable consensus has emerged on the importance of merger and separation as a key psychological conflict of the early period.

Regardless of geographical location and the nature of familial organization, the conflict between separation and merger not only dominates the life of the infant but extends itself far beyond infancy and childhood into the life of the adolescent and adult. It revolves around the struggle to become an autonomous, separate person, differentiated and distinct, and, *at the same time,* to retain one's connection to significant others—either the actual parents or their later substitutes in a protean variety of shapes and forms. For the human creature, two of life's most powerful needs are, paradoxically, to be joined and to be separate, to be related and to be independent, to be autonomous and to be connected, and it is precisely this paradoxical and in some sense contradictory thrust in human growth and development, this antithetical, two-sided incination of people, that makes human behavior so problematical, so maddeningly difficult to see and to fathom, and that brings so much confusion to the lives of individuals and societies. Ethel Person, in her wonderful book *Dreams of Love and Fateful Encounters* (1989, 132), renders the matter this way: "Without self-will there can be no psychological separation. But neither is there any highly individuated self. The self is delineated only through separation, but the sense of being separated proves impossible to bear. The solitary self feels cut off, alone, without resources. The solitary self feels impelled to merge with a new object." What Dr. Person has captured, if I may be permitted to indicate the issue still again, is that the *two* needs, to be separate and joined, independent and connected, are from a deep psychological angle *one* need neither side of which finds expression without engaging the other, like a crab going backward and forward at the same time. When the desire for merger is felt, it typically engages the need to be separate, and the need to be separate engages the wish to be connected, joined. While it is easy to write about the matter, to employ such terms as alogical, paradoxical, and antithetical, it can be most unpleasant to experience the actual conflict when it occurs, along with the inner confusion that it often engenders. I would suggest, in fact, that we have here a major source of human stress.

From the many psychoanalytic accounts of infancy and childhood and of the growth and development of the human creature, I choose what is generally regarded as the most methodologically sophisticated, accurate, and helpful, namely, Margaret Mahler's *Psychological Birth of the Human Infant* (1975). A child psychiatrist and pediatrician working with normal children in a specially constructed facility in New York City during the 1950s and 1960s, Mahler (and her associates) places the accent immediately on the struggle between separation and union.

We take for granted, she reminds us (3), our experience of ourselves as both fully "in" and fully separate from the "world out there." Our consciousness of ourselves as distinct, differentiated entities and our concomitant absoprtion into the external environment, without an awareness of self, are the polarities between which we move with varying ease, and with varying degrees of alternation or simultaneity. Yet the establishment of such consciousness, such ordinary, taken-for-granted aware- ness, is a slowly unfolding process that is not coincident in time with our biological emergence from the womb. It is tied closely and developmentally to our dawning experience of our bodies as separate in space and belonging only to us, and to our dawning experience of the primary love object as also separate in space, as having an existence of her/his own. Moreover, the struggle to achieve this "individuation" reverberates throughout the course of our lives: "It is never finished; it remains always active; new phases of the life cycle find new derivatives of the earliest proc- esses still at work" (3). As we shall see, the institutions of culture are designed in large measure to address the endless transforma- tions of these "early processes."

What must be stressed in particular here is the strength of *both sides* of the polarity. Children, with every move toward maturation, are confronted with the threat of "object loss," with traumatic situations involving separation from the caregiver. Thus they are constantly tempted to draw back, to regress, to move *toward* the object and the old relation as opposed to *away* from the object and the anticipated future, the new reality. At the same time, the normally endowed child strives mightily to emerge from his early fusion (we could say confusion) with the mother, to *escape* and to *grow*. His individuation consists pre- cisely of those developmental achievements, those increasing motor and mental accomplishments, that begin to mark his separate existence, his separate identity as a separate being. The ambivalent impulses toward and away from the object, the great urge to differentiate and at the same time stay connected, are in Mahler's words, forever intertwined (4), although they may proceed divergently, one or the other lagging behind or leaping ahead during a given period.

Mahler makes plain that this process is not merely one of many equally important processes which transpire during the early time. On the contrary, the achievement of separation con- stitutes the very core of the self (4), the foundation of one's identity and being as a person. Yet this foundation can be gained (and here is the echo of a paradox again) only if the parent gives to the child a persistent, uninterrupted feeling of connection, of union—a tie that encourages the very breaking of it. This delicate balancing act is never perfect, and Mahler emphasizes throughout the course of her study that old conflicts over separation, old, unresolved issues of identity and bodily boundaries, can be reawakened or even remain active throughout the course of one's existence, at any or all stages of the life cycle. What appears to be a struggle for connection or distinctness in the now of one's experience can be the flare up of the ancient struggle in which one's self began to emerge from the orbit of the *magna mater*. We will shortly be exploring the degree to which this last observation sheds light upon the cult of the Goddess into whose cosmic body the Witch longs to be absorbed.

By separation, then, Mahler does not mean primarily the physical separation of the baby in space or the distance from the caregiver, the kind of separation we associate, for example, with the work of John Bowlby. What Mahler has in mind is an *inward* or *intrapsychic separation* from both the mother and her extension, the world. The gradual development of this subjective awareness, this inward perception of the self and the other, leads eventually to clear, distinct inner representations of a "self" which is distinguished from "external objects." It is precisely this sense of being a separate individual that psychotic children are unable to achieve.

Similarly, when Mahler uses the term "symbiosis," the accent is not upon a behavioral state but an inward condition, a feature of primitive emotional life wherein the differentiation between the self and the mother has not occurred, or where a regression *to* an undifferentiated state has occurred. This does not necessarily require the presence of the mother; it can be based on *primitive images of oneness, or on a denial of perceptions that postulate separation.* Thus for Mahler, identity during the early period does not refer to the child having a sense of *who* he is; it refers to the child having a sense *that* he is (8). Indeed, the sense that he is can be regarded as the first step in the process of an unfolding individuality. The achievement of separation-individuation is a kind of "second birth," a "hatching" (9) from the symbiotic mother-infant "membrane" in which the child is originally contained.

The Stages of Development

Mahler calls the earliest stage of development "autistic." The infant "spends most of his day in a half-sleeping, half-waking state" (41). He awakens mainly to feed and falls to sleep again when he is satisfied, or relieved of tensions. "Physiological rather than psychological processes are dominant," and the period as a whole is "best seen" in physiological terms. There is nothing abnormal about this "autism," as Maher employs the term. The baby simply lacks awareness of the mother as a ministering agent and of himself as the object of her ministrations.[1]

From the second month on, however, the baby increasingly feels the presence of the mother, and it is just this sense of the caretaker (or the "need-satisfying object") *being there* that marks the inception of the normal symbiotic phase, which reaches a peak of intensity at about six to nine months. The most remarkable feature of this phase (and one that will be of great significance for us as we proceed with our study of Witchcraft) is contained in Mahler's point that the infant "behaves and functions as though he and his mother were an omnipotent system—a dual unity with one common boundary" (44). The symbiotic infant participates emotionally and perceptually in a kind of delusional or hallucinatory fusion with the omnipotent mothering figure. Later in infancy and childhood, and indeed later in life at all stages when we experience severe stress, "this is the mechanism to which the ego regresses." Mahler hypothesizes that the symbiotic stage is "perhaps what Freud and Romain Rolland discussed in their dialogue as the sense of boundlessness of the oceanic feeling" (44). Psychoanalytic discussions of religion, and in particular of mystical states, generally begin with a reference to the Freud-Rolland exchange.

In this way, when the autistic phase subsides, or, to use the metaphors characteristic of Mahler's treatise, when the "autistic shell" has "cracked" and the child can no longer "keep out external stimuli," a "second protective, yet selective and receptive shield" begins to develop in the form of the "symbiotic orbit," the mother and the child's dual-unity. While the normal autistic phase serves postnatal physiological growth and homeostasis, the normal symbiotic phase marks the all-important human capacity to bring the mother into a psychic fusion that comprises "the primal soil from which *all subsequent relationships form*" (48; my emphasis). We commence our existence as people in the illusion that the other (who appears to be omnipotent) is a part of the self. Although the mother is actually *out there*, ministering to the child, she is perceived by the latter to be a facet of his own organism, his own primitive ego. What the mother "magically" accomplishes in the way of care—the production of milk, the provision of warmth, the sensation of security—the baby omnipotently attributes to the mother *and to himself.* At the emotional, preverbal level, he declares, in effect, "I am not separate from my symbiotic partner; my partner and I are one. Whatever my partner appears to possess and to do, I possess and do as well. Whatever power my partner has, I also have. We are *one,* one omnipotent indestructible unit, twin stars revolving around each other in a single orbit of emotion and will." As D. W. Winnicott (1974, 13) unforgettably expresses it, the feeling of omnipotence is so strong in the infant (and so persistently clung to in the growing child when the dual-unity of the symbiotic stage begins to break down) that it is "nearly a fact."

What this means, of course, is that the *decline* of symbiosis, or the increasing awareness of separation on the part of the child, will be experienced as a *loss of self.* If union with mother means wholeness, then dis-union will mean *less* than wholeness. As Mahler phrases it elsewhere (1968, 9), the cessation of the symbiotic phase marks the "loss of the part of [one's] ego." Let us examine Mahler's account of this original human trauma (the expulsion from paradise), and let us bear in mind as we proceed, first, that the transition from symbiosis to individuation is a multifaceted, complex process that consumes the first three years of life, and second, that for many, many people the loss of omnipotent merger and the narcissistic gratification that goes with it is never entirely accepted at the deep, unconscious level. I am not suggesting that the infant's growing abilities and independence fail to provide him with satisfaction; to be sure, they do, and Mahler is careful to emphasize *both* sides of the equation—the drive to remain with and to relinquish the mother. I am suggesting only that the movement away is attended by powerful anxiety and by the irrational wish to have it *both* ways: separateness and symbiotic union. Also, as one would suspect, the babies in Mahler's study often differ dramatically in their developmental inclinations and capacities, but more of that later.

Separation Under Way

What Mahler calls the "first subphase" of "differenation" occurs "at the peak of symbiosis" when the infant is about six months old. During his more frequent periods of wakefulness, the field of his attention gradually expands "through the coming into being of outwardly directed perceptual activity" (53). No longer is the "symbiotic orbit" the exclusive focus of his limited, yet evolving "sensorium." In addition, the baby's attention gradually combines with "a growing store of memories of mother's comings and goings, of good and bad experiences" which comprise the mnemic core of what psychoanalysis calls the "good" and the "bad" object. The infant is more alert, more goal-directed, and his attendants begin to talk of his "hatching," of his emergence from the "autistic shell."

As the seventh month approaches, "there are definite signs that the baby is beginning to differentiate his own body" from that of his mother (54). "Tentative experimentation at individuation" can be observed in such behavior as "pulling at the mother's hair, ears, or nose, putting food into the mother's mouth, and straining his body away from mother in order to have a better look at her, to scan her and the environment. This is in contrast to simply moulding into mother when held." The infant's growing visual and motor powers help him to "draw his body together" (55) and to commence the construction of his own, separate ego on the basis of this bodily awareness and sensation. At times, the baby even begins to move away from the mother's enveloping arms, to resist the passive "lap babyhood" which marks the earliest months of life. As he does this, however, he constantly "checks back" to mother with his eyes. He is becoming interested in mother as "mother" and compares her with "other" people and things. He discovers what belongs and what does not belong to the mother's body—a brooch, eyeglasses, a comb. He is starting to discriminate, in short, between the mother and all that which is different from or similar to her.

This incipient individuation on the baby's part is accompanied by considerable anxiety, the most striking manifestation of which occurs in the presence of strangers. Like so much else in the area of separation-union, "stranger anxiety" evinces two distinct yet interrelated aspects. On the one hand, strangers fascinate the infant, who, in Mahler's words, shows great "eagerness to find out about them" (56). On the other hand, strangers terrify the infant by reminding him of the other-than-mother world, the world of separation, the world that appears as symbiosis and dual-unity fade. After pointing out that babies vary in their susceptibility to stranger anxiety (and other anxiety as well), Mahler offers us the example of Peter, who at eight months reacts initially with wonder and curiosity to a stranger's mild overtures for his attention. Yet, two minutes later, although he is close to his mother, even leaning against her leg, Peter bursts into tears as the stranger touches his hair (57). Such is the emotional turbulence that accompanies the onset of individuation during the first subphase.

Increasing Autonomy, Persistent Ambivalence

Mahler divides the second subphase into the early practicing period and the practicing subphase proper. During the former, the ten- to eleven-month infant becomes more and more deeply absorbed in his expanding mental and physical universe. He begins rapidly to distinguish his own body from his mother's, to actively establish a specific (as opposed to symbiotic) bond with her, and to indulge his autonomous, independent interests while in close proximity to her. In a word, he begins to *transfer* his absorption in mother to the world around him. He explores the objects in his vicinity—toys, bottles, blankets—with his eyes, hands, and mouth; his growing locomotor capacity widens his environment. Not only does he have a "more active role in determining closeness and distance to mother," but the "modalities that up to now were used to explore the relatively familiar" suddenly transport him to a new reality. There is more to see, to hear, to touch (66).

Yet in all of this, Mahler is careful to point out, the mother is "still the center of the child's universe" (66). His experience of his "new world" is "subtly related" to *her*, and his excursions into the other-than-mother realm are often followed by periods of intense clinging and a refusal to separate. For an interval the baby is absorbed in some external object and seems oblivious to mother's presence; a moment later he jumps up and rushes to her side expressing his need for physical proximity. Again and again he displays a desire for "emotional refueling" (69), that is to say, for a dose of maternal supplies—hugging, stroking, chatting—after a period of independent activity. What Mahler's children (and all children) want—and we come here to a crucial utterance—is to "move away independently" from the mother and, *at the same time,* to "remain connected" to her (70).

The practicing subphase proper (eleven to fifteen months) marks the high point of the child's move toward a separate existence. Not only does he experience a dramatic spurt in cognitive development, he also achieves what Mahler calls "the greatest step in human individuation," his upright locomotion (71).

These "precious months" of increasing powers and skills comprise "the child's love affair with the world": the "plane of his vision changes; . . . he finds unexpected and changing perspectives. . . . The world is the junior toddler's oyster. . . . Narcissism is at its peak. . . . The chief characteristic of this period is the child's great narcissistic investment in his own functions, his own body, and the objectives of his expanding reality" (71). Adding to the exhilaration, notes Mahler, is the child's "elated escape from fusion with, from engulfment by, mother." Here is the movement *away* in its most striking biological and psychological expression.

Yet even here, in the midst of this great expansion, this "love affair with the world," the paradoxical, ambivalent aspect of human development rears its head as mightily as ever in the form of deep-seated, pervasive anxiety. "The course of true love never did run smooth," observes Shakespeare, and the words would seem to apply to our earliest developmental experiences. The child's rapidly expanding ego functions bring with them both the threat of "object loss" and the fear of being "reengulfed" by the mother. One minute he expresses a need for "checking back," for "emotional refueling," for knowing exactly the mother's whereabouts; the next minute he forcibly removes himself from mother's caressing arms in an effort to assert his capacity for active, independent functioning. Sometimes the baby runs away to make sure mother *wants* to catch him up; yet when she does, he shows resentment at being held and stroked.

Even the enormous step of upright locomotion and the increase in perception that it brings to the child holds *both* sides of the dual-unity equation. It is the need for mother's emotional support at the instant he learns to walk that Mahler captures unforgettably: "The child walks alone with his eyes fixed on his mother's face, not on the difficulties in his way. . . . In the very same moment that he is emphasizing his need for her, he is proving that he can do without her." In this way, the toddler "feels the pull of separation from his mother at the same time he asserts his individuation. It is a *mixed* experience, the child demonstrating that he can and cannot do without, his mother" (73; my emphasis). As for the mother's *physical* absence during this period (she may be working, ill, etc.), it typically sparks sadness, or even depression in the infant. The "symbiotic mothering half" of the "self" is "missed" during the very subphase that is most obviously filled with the joys of separation (74).

Undeniably Alone

The entire separation-individuation process culminates at approximately thirty months in what Mahler terms "the rapprochement subphase," the period during which the infant perceives with growing clarity and certainty that he and mother are separate beings, that the old symbiosis and the narcissistic gratifications (including omnipotence) that go with it are illusory, that he is physically and psychically *alone.* Here is Mahler's (78) powerful descripton of this watershed in a person's life: "With the acquisition of primitive skills and perceptual cognitive faculties there has been an increasingly clear differention, a separation, between the intrapsychic representation of the object and the self-representation. At the very height of mastery, toward the end of the practicing period, it had already begun to dawn on the junior toddler that the world is *not* his oyster, that he must cope with it more or less on his own, very often as a relatively helpless, small, and separate individual, unable to command relief or assistance merely by feeling the need for it or by giving voice to that need" (omnipotence). We may note, parenthetically at this juncture, that much magical and religious activity is designed to *deny* precisely this momentous event, and not only deny it but bring about its *reversal* through just those mechanisms that Mahler mentions here, namely, "mere feeling" (wishing) and "giving voice" (prayers and invocations). During the course of the next chapter we will explore these denials and reversals in great depth.

With the erosion of symbiosis, the "fear of losing the *love* of the object" (78), as opposed to losing the object, makes itself felt increasingly in the child. Up to this point (the rapprochement subphase) the object and the self have been more or less psychically indistinguishable. Now, as differentiation occurs in earnest, the object's love becomes the focus of the child's attention. This does not mean that the original anxiety over loss of the object as a part of the self disappears. It means only that an additional, more conscious or even cognitive anxiety has been superimposed upon the original, primal dread. Accordingly, the toddler begins to demand the mother's constant attention. He is deeply preoccupied with her whereabouts. He expresses enormous anger and anxiety at her leave-taking, and anguish at being left behind. He clings to mother, seeks her lap, and may begin to show a dependent interest in maternal substitutes. In a thousand ways he attempts to coerce the mother into fulfilling his wishes. He tries at times to be magnificently separate, omnipotent, rejecting: he will gain the mother's love and attention by showing her the proverbial "cold shoulder." At other times he plays the helpless baby. For weeks on end his wooing of mother alternates sharply with his expressions of resentment and outrage (97).

How do the mothers react to all this? "Some cannot accept the child's demandingness; others are unable to face the child's gradual separation, the fact that the child can no longer be regarded as part of her" (78). Yet, whatever the relational dynamics happen to be, they cannot stop the process: "no matter how insistently the toddler tries to coerce the mother, she and he can no longer function effectively as a dual unit—that is to say, the child can no longer maintain his delusion of parental omnipotence, which he still at times expects will restore the symbiotic status quo." The child must "gradually and painfully give up the delusion of his own grandeur, often by way of dramatic fights with mother—less so, it seemed to us, with father. This is the crossroads of what we term the rapprochement crisis" (79). Mahler observes in a sentence at which we prick up our ears as we near the study of Witchcraft that "many uniquely human problems and dilemmas" which are "sometimes never completely resolved during the entire life cycle" have their origin here, during the end of symbiosis and the onset of separation (100).

Resolving the Dilemma

The resolution of the rapprochement crisis comes about in a variety of ways, the description of which concludes the first half of Mahler's study. As the child experiences a growing capacity to be alone, his clamoring for omnipotent control starts to diminish. He shows less separation anxiety, fewer alternating demands for closeness and autonomy. Not only does he begin to understand empathetically what his mother is going through, which allows him to "unify the good and bad objects into one whole representation" (110), but he begins to identify with the problems and struggles of the youngsters around him. In this way, he begins to turn to other people, and in many instances to his own father, in his effort to satisfy his needs. And with the wholesale emergence of gender differences, he starts to participate in those activities that are peculiar to his/her sex.

Equally important, the child's capacity for verbalization and symbolization begins to lead him toward the cultural realm, toward an endless variety of substitutive, or, in Winnicott's (1974, 118) famous expression, "transitional" objects that characteristically take the form of "blankies," storybooks, toys, pets, and so on, and that exist somewhere "between the child's fantasies and reality," in what Winnicott calls "transitional space." We might say that the child's growing ability to incorporate the world into his burgeoning ego leads him to a series of new internalizations, new inward presences, which are appropriate to his age and to the problems he confronts. He is beginning to live with his own thoughts and with the companions of his inner world. This is what we usually mean by "being alone."

In the majority of cases and generally for all normal children, such developments culminate in the establishment of what Mahler calls "object constancy" (110), and with it, the inception of an individuated life. By "object constancy" Mahler has in mind "the presence of a reliable internal image that remains relatively stable irrespective of the state of instinctual need or inner discomfort. On the basis of this achievement, temporary separation can be lengthened and better tolerated" (110). This is the necessary step, the vital inward accomplishment, that permits further growth, further individuation, and further ego strength in the preschooler and eventually in the school child.

Mahler devotes the second half of her treatise to several lengthy case histories in which we see children struggling from normal autism and symbiosis to separation and individuation. She strives in these sections to illustrate her theoretical position at the clinical level, the level from which the theoretical materials originally arose, of course. As she does this, Mahler makes clear something that she stresses in many places in Part One, namely that it is the *combination* of a particular caretaker interacting with a particular child that ultimately shapes the child's emerging character in terms of both conscious and unconscious processes. Projections pass not only from the baby to the mother, but from the mother to the baby as well. "It seemed that the ability to cope with separateness, as well as with actual physical separation," declares Mahler (103), "was dependent in each case on the history of the mother-child relationship, as well as on its present state. We found it hard to pinpoint just what it was in the individual cases that produced more anxiety in some and an ability to cope in others. Each child had established by this time his own characteristic ways of coping." Thus, when we look at the whole picture, we spy an element of mystery, a unique, intangible quality that pertains to each mother-infant bond and that can never be fully explained by observers, or indeed by the mother and infant who are involved in the relationship. What occurs early on is not strictly an enigma but it has its enigmatic aspect, and we must always bear this in mind. Human behavior finally escapes whatever logical space we try to fit it into. Reality *happens,* from the *inside,* and can never be perfectly reconstructed.

As I suggested on several occasions in the context, the struggle for and against separation extends itself powerfully not only into ritualistic behaviors such as Witchcraft but into the nature and development of our perceptual lives generally, including the whole of culture. Although it may appear a bit strange to express the matter thus, our ordinary consciousness in the widest, most all-inclusive sense is inextricably bound up with the early struggle over separation *and cannot be grasped apart from it.* We must remember as we move through the next few pages that what Mahler describes in the final paragraphs of her theoretical section is the passing of the rapprochement crisis, *not* the passing of the separation-union conflict. Indeed, it is the thesis of this book, and has been from the outset, that this conflict *never ceases,* that it so forcefully shapes and directs our conduct as to gain a place among the central conflicts of our experience as a form of life.

As Mahler herself makes clear (115), a "sound image" of the maternal figure does not mean that the old longing for merger stops, that the fear of reengulfment goes away, that anxiety, ambivalence, and splitting suddenly vanish, along with feelings of omnipotence and narcissistic grandiosity; it does not mean that the primal terrors of rejection and loss miraculously disappear forever. The establishment of a sound maternal image simply means that the little person can stumble ahead *still loaded* with the great, absorbing issues of the early time, still loaded with the stress that attends the erosion of symbiosis, still wishing contradictorily for both merger and differentiation, and still smarting from the collapse of dual-unity. What occurs as the infant undergoes separation has been described by Dr. Ana-Maria Rizzuto (1979, 49) as a "life-long mourning process that triggers an endless search for replacement." To express the matter from a different yet crucially related angle, the passing of the rapprochement crisis simply means that one is now in a position to act out among others this basic human dilemma, this rooted, unconscious issue as it manifests itself projectively at the levels of both individual and group conduct. It means that one can now seek for omnipotence, fusion, and narcissistic gratification in the wider world. In a manner of speaking, one is loose. The old cliché that we are all more or less neurotic hopefully emerges with fresh clarity at this juncture.

Let us deepen and enrich Mahler's findings, then, and conclude our psychoanalytic investigation of origins, by concentrating once more on the first years of life, this time with ordinary consciousness itself as the focus.

Construction of the Inner Realm

It boils down to this: From the beginning of our existence we *internalize* the world; we take experiential events into our emerging mind-body, and we do this fully, deeply, and finally at the level of ganglionic-synaptic development itself. If the reader is wondering why the early period is so crucial, so all-determining for our later lives, this is where the answer begins to emerge, in the psychodynamics of human internalization. "Mind is born early in life," writes Jose Delgado (1971, 26), "as an infant is attracted to sources of comfort and repelled by sources of distress." Even when we are thinking logically as adults, even when we are indulging in the "pure reason" that we associate with philosophers such as Descartes and Kant, the legacy of our early years is there, humming beneath the surface, as it were. If one can think of the multifaceted human ego as a group of actors standing on a stage, one will understand "pure reason" as a mental request that everyone move out of the way so that "reason" may preside at the center. The cooperative members of the cast may do this, *but they do not leave the stage,* and they *influence* "reason" by their continued presence there. The living organism, in other words, always *perceives* the world with the whole mind, as opposed to thinking about it with only a part of the mind. Perception, not thinking, is primary.

Of the powerful internalizing that we do toward the inception of our lives, that which involves the caretaker (usually the mother) is of enormous significance. As developmental psychologists express it, the *object* (this term is used, remember, because the caretaker is not yet perceived by the baby as a person) "enters the infant's dawning psyche" as the deep internalization of life's earliest phase, and she "persists there as a presence, later to become an image" during the period in which verbalization begins. This interplay between mother and infant is "directly involved in the shaping of the infant's personality." Intuitive or feeling perception "begins with maximal intensity at birth as the baby becomes subject in a structuring way to the maternal attitude" (Rheingold 1964, 30). So intense, so pervasive, and so basic is this interaction between mother and child that we would do well to regard the mother herself not as a distinct entity but as a kind of organ of the baby. It is in the growth of this unique union that we find the nucleus of human identity.

The Mirror

The genesis and the formation of the self derive from the baby's initial mirroring experience with the mother. For the past few decades this remarkable aspect of our origins has been studied intensively and has come to be regarded as a central feature of our development. The investigations of Rene Spitz (1965, 81) and his associates during the 1950s and 1960s established at the clinical level the baby's inclination to concentrate on the mother's face—and in particular on her eyes—during periods of feeding. For three, or perhaps four, months the nursing infant does not look at the mother's breast (or at the bottle held close to her breast) but at her face. "From the moment the mother comes into the room to the end of nursing he stares at her face." What is especially interesting in this regard is the connection between such primal gazing and the mouth, or "oral cavity."

While the child takes into his mouth and body his physical nourishment, he takes into his dawning awareness or his "visceral brain" the emotional, psychological materials that he discoves in the face, eyes, and bodily attitude of the mother. It is often remarked that the first ego is a body ego and that our later life is influenced at the perceptual level by the foundational experiences our bodies undergo as consciousness awakens. We have here a compelling instance of how this works. When Spitz calls the "oral cavity" in its conjunction with the mother's body "the cradle of human perception," he reminds us that sucking in and spitting out are the first, the most basic, and the most persistent *perceptual* behaviors among humans. They underlie at the bodily level our subsequent rejections and acceptances, our subsequent negations and celebrations, of experience.

Although Spitz established the baby's inclination to stare at the mother's face, notes H. M. Southwood (1973, 235–39), whose discussion I will follow closely here, he did not state that mother and infant spend considerable time looking at each other, nor did he contend that such looking, along with the mother initiating the infant's facial expressions and sounds, provided the means for the baby to regard the mother's face and sounds as his own. An inborn tendency on the part of the infant prompts him to seek out his mother's gaze and to do so regularly and for extended periods. The mother, because of tendencies developed during the course of her relationship with her own mother, sets about exploiting this mutual face-gazing activity. As the eye-to-eye contact becomes frequent, and easily observed by the investigator, the mother's inclination to continually change her facial expression, as well as the quality of her vocalizing, emerges with striking clarity. Usually she smiles and nods and coos; sometimes in response to an infant frown she frowns. In virtually every instance the mother's facial and vocal behavior comprises an imitation of the baby's.

Thus, as the mother descends to the infant's level, she provides him with a particular kind of human reflection. She does not simply give the baby back his own self; she reinforces a portion of the baby's behavior in comparison with another portion. She gives the baby back not merely a part of what he is doing but something of her own in addition. In individual development, "the precursor of the mirror is the mother's face" (Winnicott 1974, 130). The upshot may be stated as follows: The kind of behavior we connect with the ego or the perceptual apparatus derives in large measure from the behavior of the mother. Not only does she trigger the ego's formation, she determines the kind of stimuli to which the child will attend, including the stimuli that will eventually come through language.

The entire developmental sequence has been captured in detail by Daniel Stern (1977). For the infant, hundreds of "experiential units" are strung together and occur over and over again during each interaction, every day. The infant has the opportunity to internalize each "unit" as a separate representation. At the level of neuronic processes, of course, these internalizations become an integral part of the human mind-brain. In other words, they trigger memory traces and get stored. For a "unit" to become internalized there must be a physical, a cognitive, and an emotional aspect to the experience. When these are in place assimilation occurs. At the foundation level of our perceptual nature, cognition and emotion cannot be treated separately, or compartmentalized. We begin and we continue as human beings to "sees the world feelingly," as Gloucester puts it in *King Lear.* Although such feeling may be scarcely discernable, or even totally concealed by one's attitude toward the world, it is there.

Our mental makeup, then, is shaped by those with whom we entered into "object relations" during the early phases of our development. Our earliest "objects" become dynamic parts of our personality structure and continue to influence us in all that we do long after the specific persons who were the aim of our internalizing tendency have ceased to be. By the time we have reached adulthood there exists within us an inner world, a kind of psychic universe which is inhabited by the "objects" that have entered us, or more properly, that we have taken into ourselves along our maturational way. *We live in two worlds,* from the beginning, and our perceptual life must be regarded as a function of the interaction of these worlds which continually impinge upon one another.

The Dark Side of the Mirror: Splitting

We are beginning to understand the psychological direction from which our ordinary awareness arises. To do this more fully, however, we must grasp the two-sided, or "split" nature of our early, foundational experience, something that Mahler touched upon during the course of her investigations.

On the one hand, many of the "representational units" which the baby takes in contribute to his contentment. The mother gives him a positive, nurturing introduction to existence. She soothes him, reassures him, delights him; she develops his confidence, his enthusiasm, his "joy in life." In a word, she triggers his participation in "good" materials. On the other hand, many of the "units" that are assimilated by the growing child are disruptive, or, in a very special sense, *negative* in quality.

As the child goes about building up his good maternal representation, as he gradually enlarges those aspects of the caretaker that will serve as the perceptual basis for his positive participation in the world, he confronts of necessity the imperfections of the symbiotic relationship in which he is involved. No matter how solicitous the mother is, the infant is fated to undergo tension, frustration, discomfort, and even a certain amount of pain. Such experiences mobilize anxiety. Indeed, very young infants display identical patterns of anxious behavior when they discover themselves in frightening situations, and when they are in contact with the caretaker during a period in which she is tense, angry, disquieted, or anxious herself. Repeated, inescapable exposure to inconsistent conduct prompts the developing baby to *split* the caretaker into a "good" and a "bad object" and to *internalize* these objects into a part or aspect of his perceiving self. The collection of people which each of us harbors within, carries about, and projects into our reality, reaches back in every instance to the first pair of our personifications: the good mother and the bad or evil mother. With the passage of time these early, primitive personifications get transmuted into the good me, the bad me, and the ambiguous, dreadful not me (Rheingold 1964, 164).

We must remember here that the mother's inconsistency is a grave, disruptive event for the child, that it corresponds to his worst imaginings and fears. The postponement of gratification from its mother's supplies constitutes for the infant a trauma, and residues of the infant's reaction to this trauma can be found in the psychology of later years. Because he is simply not able to *integrate* the mother's two sides, her "bad" and "good" aspects, the infant attempts to *coordinate* them by splitting and then dealing with the splits. He declares, in effect, "*mother* is not bad. There just happens to be this bad mother who appears once in a while. She and mother are not really the same person, for *mother* is always good and will never hurt and disappoint. I am obliged to interact with both *mother* and the other one" (author's quotation). Only later, when the child achieves Mahler's "object constancy," will he be able to accept goodness and badness in the same person.

Thus threats to our narcissistic integrity, to our primitive emotional and bodily self-esteem, exist from the inception of our psychic lives and stem from the interaction of the child's wishes and needs with the demands and frustrations of the external world. Such narcissistic wounds may evoke feelings of depression and a growing sense of perplexity which is frequently answered with aggressive behavior. The infant's mere inability to influence, predict, or comprehend an event which he expected on the basis of his previous experience to be able to control or understand is registered as trauma. Because the infant's thought, the whole of his primitive mentation, is tied inextricably to the mother, her mere absence through temporary departure can leave the infant with the terrible feeling that he is *empty,* empty in his mind and emotions. We may have here the deep origin and most basic, enduring expression of the feeling that one is "losing one's mind." We also now realize that the parents' very power over the life and death of the child is perceived as threatening, and internalized to become part of everyone's susceptibility to nightmare, everyone's residual paranoia. Odd as it may sound to express it this way, merely being born human is a major source of stress. In the words of Michael Eigen (1985, 329), "fragmentation and division are as much a part of our starting point as union and continuity."

The Jungian researches of Erich Neumann (1970, 148) are helpful on this score, particularly as they make explicit reference to the figure of the bad Witch. The symbolism of the "Terrible Mother," he writes, "draws its images from the inside," that is, the "bad object" appears in fantastic, ghastly forms that do not originate in the environment. Whether we are in "Egypt or India, Mexico or Etruria, Bali or Rome," we confront the archetypal expression of these intra-psychic "monsters." In the tales and myths of "all peoples, ages, and countries," as well as in our own nightmares, "witches, vampires, ghouls and spectres assail us, all terrifyingly alike." It is the internalizing of this bad object that explains our emotional fear of death. At issue here is not death as the adult conceives it, but a threat of a quality and magnitude beyond the adult's imagination. We get a glimpse of it in states of panic and in the momentary probe into infancy that some individuals experience during the course of psychotherapy (Rheingold 1964). Thus the struggle between the forces of life and death, which is inherent in the biologically precarious infantile condition, becomes involved in the infant's response to the mother that protects and satisfies and to the mother that frustrates and deprives. Where the fear of death is concerned, it is the uncertain ties to the living world at all ages that shake us more than the awareness of biological cessation (Steinzor 1979).

What I am maintaining is that we cannot understand the complex symbol that death comprises for the human creature, or the powerful role of death-consciousness in the impulse toward religious belief (including, of course, neo-paganism) if we exclude from the discussion the primal anxiety of the early period. Because the mother's impact on the child is preverbal, because her presence is internalized before higher conceptualization begins, it is very, very difficult to subject our split foundations to reason. True, as Mahler points out, there is a diminution of splitting during the rapprochement subphase when the child becomes more empathetic to the mother's position. But as I have suggested, this marks only a diminution (sometimes a temporary one) that permits the rapprochement crisis to pass. It does not even begin to mean that the human tendency to splitting has ceased. On the contrary, our anxious obsession with death, as well as our dangerous indulgence in rigid, dichotomous views of the world, with the good guys over here and the bad guys over there, is rooted largely in the primitive splitting of the early time which leaves perdurable traces on our "normal" perception.

The Sands of Time and the Container of Space

The influence of the foundational years reaches right down into the most basic aspects of our ordinary consciousness. For example, there is virtually unanimous agreement among developmental psychologists that our sense of time or duration, which underlies perceptually everything we do, originates in the anxious stress of the mother-child relationship (cf. Hartocollis 1974). What is crucial for us to remember here is the tight connection between the needy infant's posture of anticipation, the change it produces in the caretaker, the resulting stimulation of the infant, and the growth of temporal awareness. I am not suggesting that the baby possesses an organized time sense. I am suggesting, rather, that immediately after his emergence from the womb innate factors become subsumed in the mother-child dialogue and hence colored by the powerful emotions that characterize that dialogue. What was biological becomes psychological, experienced in the child's developing ego as part of the link to the gradually emerging parental figure.

The imperfect pattern of the child's needs and the mother's availability prompts the infant to protect himself from frustration by *anticipating* the fulfillment of his wishes. Time is subjectively experienced as separation from the nourishing object, a traumatic event, and as fantasied reunion (Arlow 1984). This anticipation is closely tied to the infant's primitive, bodily awareness of change, and the awareness of change, as William James (1890) pointed out to us long ago, is the most rudimentary or primitive condition on which our sense of a time flow depends.

In this way, if our perception is tied categorically to our sense of duration, and if our sense of duration is tied psychologically to motivational processes involving the caregiver, then time and the caregiver, time and the internalized object, are not merely connected at the deepest level of our being but connected in a *conflictual* way. For the infant to experience time as such it is necessary that he go through a process in which he experiences the mother as both need-fulfilling and frustrating. He is both gratified and *made to wait* for food and for care generally. The waiting is sometimes a torment. The gratification is sometimes a blissful release. These are the foundational facts that underlie our symbolic notions of infinity—infinite woe, infinite bliss, and all the variations and nuances we encounter in the realms of ordinary and nonordinary reality.

Like time, space is closely associated with the first relationship. Indeed, psychic space comprises a kind of container which can be originally connected to the maternal caretaking function and to the absorption of infantile fantasies and fears. The capacity to experience space is a primary aspect of the ego, which seems to have emerged from sensations upon the foetal skin at birth, thereby awakening the skin, with its sense receptors, into its function as a surface, as a boundary between self and nonself, and as a container of the self. Without the development of such a psychic space there can be, quite simply, no perception (Grotstein 1978).

The baby's nonverbalized feelings often discover their expression through the skin: It may itch, weep, rage, and so forth. Such exigencies will be dealt with by the mother according to her ability to accept and soothe the blemished infant who will, in turn, internalize the experience. The mother demonstrates how the containing figure, herself, is experienced concretely as a skin. It is precisely this function that triggers the rudimentary idea of external and internal space (Pines 1980).

The defensive strategies of the early time are formed within levels of spatial representation which are the cognitive matrix out of which defensive strategies arise. When we withdraw, we withdraw to some place, some psychic place, that allows us to withdraw there. We split the maternal figure off to another place which permits us to split it off. We reduce the world to a space in which we dwell securely, our substitute womb of enumerated types. The very notion of separateness implies exclusion and boundaries which establish the end of one individual and the beginning of another. When the French philosopher Gaston Bachelard (1969, 5) reminds us that "all really inhabited space bears the essence of the notion of home," he only calls to mind the connection between spatial representation and the problem of mothering, for all notions of home bear the essence of the notion of mother.

The Tie to the Culture

As we have seen, the child's frantic efforts to resolve the rapprochement crisis culminate in his ability to create an entire symbolical universe and to have it inside himself in a space that Winnicott (1974) calls transitional—the word transition indicating the movement away from the caregiver and toward the wider world. In favorable circumstances or when mothering is "good enough" to prompt ordinary development, the child's potential space becomes filled with the products of his own creative imagination. If he is given the chance, the baby will begin to live creatively and to use actual objects to be creative into. If he is not given the chance, then there is no area in which the baby may have play, or may have cultural experience; then there is no link with the cultural inheritance, and no contribution to the cultural pool (ibid).

Here is the process in some detail. The "good-enough mother" begins by adapting almost completely to the infant's needs. As time goes on, "she adapts less and less completely according to the infant's growing ability to deal with her failure through his own experience." If all goes well, the infant can actually gain from his frustration by developing his own idiosyncratic style of relative independence. What is essential is that the mother give the baby, through her good-enough care, "the illusion that there is an external reality that corresponds to the infant's own capacity to create." It is precisely within this area of creativity that the infant will begin to make his transition away from the maternal figure by choosing "transitional objects"—blankets, teddy bears, story books—which afford him the magical or illusory belief that he is moving toward, or staying with, the caretaker at the same time that he is moving away from her or giving her up. Such magic, illusion, and creativity provide the child with his primary link to the "cultural realm," to the religious, artistic, and scientific symbols that comprise the shared, illusory reality of grown-ups. In this way, there is a direct development from transitional concerns to playing, and from playing to shared playing, and from this to cultural experience (1974, 12).

On the one hand, then, our ability to make symbols, to imagine, to create, and to use our powerful brains, is an innate ability that is nourished into production by maternal care. On the other hand, however, that ability is prodded into action by the very real problem of maternal separation. In the development of symbolic thought, and in the perceptual style that arises from it, there is an element of that rooted anxiety which we have been describing all along. Thus Geza Roheim's famous contention that culture itself, at the deepest psychological level, is a way back to the parent, a symbolic connection to the early time, rings true. Thinking, says Roheim (1971, 131) is deeply rooted in the emotions, and between thinking and the emotions the mental image magically resides. It means *both* away from the object (separation accomplished) and back to the object (separation overcome). Civilization originates "in delayed infancy, and its function is security." It is a "huge network of more or less successful attempts to protect mankind against the danger of object-loss, the colossal efforts made by a baby who is afraid of being left alone in the dark." I would suggest that the life of ordinary consciousness in culture is not merely a dream but a projective dream, one that invariably projects the objects of the inner world upon the objects of the environment. We do not perceive the world subjectively—the customary claim—but *objectively* in the sense that includes the parental figures as the target of the infant's desires. Projection is a feature of everyday awareness, and more than that, it holds materials from the deep and conflictual past, including the separation stage. All mental presentations are actively perceptual. We meet the sense impression halfway. From early infancy on, whenever we mentally attend, classify, anticipate, orient, or understand, we project.

The Word

Nearly half a century ago, the pioneering investigations of the Russian linguist Vygotsky (1979) made clear that the development of language was not primarily a cognitive process (the orthodox view) but an interactive, social process loaded with emotional, bodily components from the preverbal period. Because thought and speech develop in a parallel and reciprocal fashion, we must ultimately think of language as a dynamic system of meaning in which the emotional and the intellectual unite. The egocentric speech of the three-year-old does not disappear when the child reaches seven or eight. Instead of atrophying, such egocentric speech goes underground, that is, it turns into inner speech and forms the foundation of that inward babble which, joined to higher cognitive components, comes eventually to comprise a sizeable portion of our ordinary consciousness. In this way, the development of thinking is not from the individual to the social but from the social to the individual. The child starts conversing with himself as he has been doing with others.

As for the spoken word, it is initially a substitute for the gesture, for the bodily attitude and bodily expression that precede the verbalized sound. When the child says "mama," it is not merely the word that means, say, put me in the chair, but the child's whole behavior at that moment, his reaching out for the chair, trying to hold it, etc. In contrast to the egocentric speech that goes inward, verbalized speech goes outward; the child uses it as a method of pointing. It is the fusion of this inward speech and developing outward speech that finally comprises human thought in its ordinary, basic expression.

We appreciate from this viewpoint the growing psychological realization, based explicitly on Vygotsky's work, that thinking is an unconscious process in the first instance (Basch 1971). Even our conscious speech, the psychological community has come to recognize, is pervaded by unconscious mechanisms to the degree that it is tied to our thinking (Roustang 1976). This means that our thinking, our stream of consciousness itself in the most general, all-inclusive sense, is the source of those slips of the tongue on which Freud stumbled nearly a century ago.

With regard to the role of *separation* in all of this, we must note that symbol formation (or word formation) arises from the infant's shared experience with the mother (Bleich 1970). The common act of "referential pointing" starts with the mother's invitation but soon leads to the child inviting the mother to join in the contemplation of some object. This marks the beginning of what psychologists call "intellectual stereoscopy" in which the objectification of the world is dependent on social interaction. The child names things *to* someone, and the loving feedback he receives becomes the incentive for naming further things. The whole idea of two-ness and separateness arises from this mutuality. Thus the presence and absence of the mother and of important physical objects in the child's world play motivational roles in the development of representational thought.

In fact, the ability to recognize mother, to conceptualize her as mother, is goaded into existence by the need to cope with her absence, or loss. The feeling of loss becomes the motive for "acquiring the capacity to represent absent objects or to represent objects regardless of their presence or absence." When the baby names the absent object, he predicates it on the basis of its former presence: thus, mommy gone. The same act can predicate a future presence on a current absence. The ideas of gone and mommy are linked and placed in relation to one another (Bleich 1970). The whole business of linguistic predication is thus associated with the problem of separation from the caretaker. Again, as the child links up mommy and gone, he creates a dependent relationship between two ideas that substitutes for each idea's dependency on actual experience. This gives the child the power to recall the mother at will. Symbolic representation (as we saw in Winnicott's discussion of play) comes to comprise a way back to the missing object of one's emotions.

Because the verbal representation of the thing is the culmination of the symbolic process, the word is the magical tie that reunites us with the all-important figure(s) of infancy and childhood. It is not merely that maternal stimulation during the time of language development is necessary for the fulfillment of the child's potential; our symbolic seeing is charged with the emotional energy that went into our life and death struggle to maintain our connection to the caregiver at the same time we were giving her up. Through the early imperfections of mothering we learn to grip the world with our bodies, with our tense anticipation (the time sense). Through the crises of separation, which continue to transpire after the early period, we learn to grip the world with our minds, with our symbols, with our *words*. The mirror phase of infancy eventually gives way to the representational mirror of a mind that has separation on its mind. The very running on of our thoughts in ordinary consciousness becomes a link to the figures of the past.

The problem, of course, is that these figures recall not only the good side of our early existence but the bad side as well, the side that is loaded with frustration, rage, envy, anxiety, and disappointment, the side that speaks for the ambivalence of the primary years. Moreover, no matter how bad the internalized object is, the wish for reunion persists. Indeed, the internalization of particularly bad materials paradoxically increases the intensity of that wish.

The Oedipus, and After

Internalization of stress does not cease with the close of the primary years. On the contrary, the newcomer emerges from this turbulent period to confront the strain of the oedipal phase during which the emotional and sensual desire for the parent of the opposite sex creates a fear of castration in the male child (we will come to the female in a moment), as well as powerful feelings of ambivalence and jealousy toward the male parent.

This is a time of great anxiety for the boy whose dilemma will be imperfectly and paradoxically resolved through identification with the father. That is to say, perceiving the hopelessness of removing his rival, the child begins to identify with him (identification is a form of internalization) and to strive and compete in the male world of which the father is the chief representative. As his wounded narcissism benefits from his boyish accomplishments and interactions, he gradually adopts the male point of view. Typically, his wishes and aims are now bound up with heroic achievements, glory, domination; yet the wish for the mother persists at the deepest levels, and a conflicted dependency on the father develops as a refuge from separation and loss.

The entire syndrome—to use the presently popular term—finds its expression in romantic and/or authoritarian fantasies and behaviors. As males, we go through life longing for the perfect woman (which means for mother), fearing emasculation at the hands of both women and men, identifying with symbols of power and control (the nation, the leader, the company, the winning team, wealth), and making the best of what we perceive to be our failures and shortcomings. It is a pathetic picture, and would even be ridiculous were it not so replete with deep and genuine discontentment. When, thousands of years ago, the Buddha bluntly maintained that life is suffering, he probably had some ancient version of this syndrome in mind.

For the female child the dynamics of the oedipal phase are rather different; the stress that results, however, can be just as intense. If a single utterance had to be made to get at the essentials of the matter, it would point out that the girl's partial absorption (as opposed to the boy's almost total absorption) into the father's socially oriented universe during the resolution of the oedipal crisis leaves the female child more directly and uninterruptedly in the midst of the preoedipal, maternally centered issues that characterize the first years of life. Hence the girl is more prone than the boy to evince open, ongoing concern with "boundary issues," or issues of separation and merger, and to regard the male parent (and his later substitues) not so much as an avenue away from the mother's world as a means of resolving problems inextricably tied to the imperfections of the mother's care.

In even briefer compass, girls (and women) remain absorbed in the issue of closeness, and when girls (and women) discover themselves involved with normal males who fear such closeness, whose pursuits have been directed away from precisely such closeness, the old, familiar tension between the sexes results. Women tend to experience confusion when the needs of the self, particularly the assertive, aggressive self, clash with the need to preserve and enhance relationships, to express care and concern. Men, placing the emphasis on separation and achievement, typically experience less confusion as the needs of the self arise during periods of interpersonal and professional crisis, but they may also harbor an underlying sense of isolation, a loneliness and disconnectedness that often plagues them throughout the course of their lives. We will see how a cult such as Wicca addresses these basic issues of identity and gender.

Several years after the close of the oedpial period adolescence brings forth its weighty issues: genital sexuality, increasing separation from the parental presence, the forging of a consistent, integrated character, and a growing awareness of adult imperfections. It is a formidable list, and for millions, a hellish time, exacerbated today by a decline of familial support and cohesion, by a world of impersonal technological forces and influences, by an increasingly unhealthful, polluted environment (adult failure at the stewardship of the planet), and by the annihilative, "doomsday" weaponry of the world's "great powers." Of course neither oedipal nor adolescent issues are strictly *perceptual* ones, as the issues of the mirror and separation stages are. By the age of six, and obviously by the age of twelve or thirteen, the perceptual apparatus in its underlying, unconscious essentials is complete. Indeed, the oedipal period and adolescence characteristically inherit, and are shaped by, the problems and forces of the foundational years (cf. Dorpat 1988). And that is the point. The stress of the later dilemmas deepens the primal, mind-body anxiety that we have been describing in the context. Our projective style of perceiving the world is considerably intensified as oedipal and adolescent conflicts absorb the struggles of the early time.

Qualifications and Reaffirmations: A Final Preparatory Word

The question arises: Does the generalized model that I have presented thus far apply to all children, in all families, in all cultures, in our rapidly changing world? No one will deny that children, mothers, fathers, and families vary considerably in regard to developmental tendencies and interrelational styles. Mahler herself is careful to point out again and again that quality of response and rate of maturation differ dramatically among her youthful subjects and that such difference is compounded by the uniqueness of each parent and each familial situation. Recently, Mary Ainsworth (1983) and her associates have confirmed that babies do not react uniformly to specifically the problem of physical separation. For some, the departure or the absence of the caretaker is far more traumatic than it is for others. As for reunion, some children are reluctant to "make up" for a lengthy period; others are happily in their parent's arms right away. Yet the separation-union conflict is there to one degree or another in all children, all parents, and all families. We know babyhood and symbiosis at the beginning; later, we know individuation and relative autonomy. Mahler's "phases," and the issues that pertain to them, appear to be universal.

Accordingly, when we apply the model in the present case, we will find that certain points are particularly relevant to certain Witches and rituals, and that other points pertain especially to other practitioners and rites. We will discover that some Witches are more susceptible to problems of separation and union than other Witches are. The psychoanalytic approach will be very significant here and not very significant there. Some aspects of the Craft may escape us altogether. The point is, our model will be strong enough to tell us a great deal about modern Witchcraft, and that is all we can expect from it. To demand absolute relevance and certainty in regard to each and every ritual and each and every member of the Wiccan community would be perverse. The inexact human sciences simply do not work that way. In the end, we do the best we can with the data that we have, and we leave it to those who come later to improve upon our findings. This is called "the dialectical method."

Similar reflections may be brought to bear when Peter Neubauer (1985) informs us that the mother is not always the central presence during the early period, that our rapidly changing culture increasingly witnesses the father (and others) assuming a pivotal role. Undoubtedly this is so. But even here, where fathers or uncles or nannies or aunts are conspicuous, the issue of separation-union will still be crucial for the developing child. Motivational dynamics may shift direction, yet the scheme that Mahler gives us will continue to disclose essential conflicts and provide a useful foundation. I am not denying that future decades may require wholesale reformulation; I am only suggesting that we should continue to make theories, based on our best evidence, while the world around us continues to change. What choice *have* we, after all? Were we to wait for change to stop so that we could begin to make theories, we would never make any theories.

With regard to cross-cultural issues, which we can only apprehend as formidable, we must remember, first, that the Witchcraft movement as we know it today is overwhelmingly a Western phenomenon and thus very hospitable to Mahler's scheme, along with the expansion of it that we have undertaken in this chapter. Second, psychoanalytic studies of maturational problems among non-Western peoples reveal, on the one hand, the enormous differences at work in the world, and on the other, the ubiquity of the separation-union conflict.

East Indians, for example, struggle mightily to achieve a coherent, separate self amidst a consuming and often maddening network of familial ties and responsibilities (Roland 1988). The Japanese struggle similarly with the powerful demands of the work group, a conformist, authoritarian extension of the original family structure (ibid.). And the struggles of *both* these peoples are complicated and deepened by the arrival of Western, often American, ideas and attitudes. Yet for all the differences, which I do not for one minute propose to minimize, we still see the basic, core conflict over union and separation as it emerges from Mahler and as it may be cautiously extrapolated to the adolescents and adults of other societies. Indeed, this primal struggle exists worldwide and is perhaps best illustrated in Eli Sagan's (1985) recent study of various cultures—each of which appears to be negotiating a stage of Mahler's scheme.

Maintaining that "the psyche is the paradigm for the development of culture and society," and following closely Mahler's depiction of psychic development, Sagan views the human community as a whole passing from a) early kinship organizations rooted in the familial bond, to b) complex organizations based on chieftainship and comprising the first, wrenching move *away* from kinship, to c) monarchic and archaic civilizations (Egypt, China) based on the elaborate, hierarchical arrangements that ensure individual security through stable social order. Sagan writes,

Society may choose to resist . . . the drive toward development, but once advance is resolved upon, society is not free to take any direction ... it wants. No primitive society develops into an archaic or classical civilization. Every primitive society that embarks on a developmental journey becomes a complex society. The logic within this advance is not primarily economic, or scientific, or even rational; ... it is primarily a psychological logic. The stages in development from primitive to chieftainship to early monarchies to complex monarchies to archaic civilizations are projections and magnifications onto society as a whole of stages in the development of the psyche. The journey of the psyche through the various phases in the process of separation and individuation is recapitulated in social development. (364)

As for the advanced, democratic society in which we exist today, it is "the least dependent upon fundamental kinship ties of any political system ever invented" (375). For Sagan, then, the developmental conflict described by Mahler is not only ubiquitous for the individual but for the group as well; the *world* struggles with problems of merger and separation, with the clashing needs for cohesion and personal, independent expression. With all of this in mind, let us turn to the Witches.

3

A Psychoanalysis of Witchcraft Today

Part One: The Texts, The Tenets, the Rituals

The Craft, as we know it today, has a maddeningly complex, disputatious history capable of discouraging the most sanguine investigator. Some adherents point to Sir James Frazer as the founding father, others to Margaret Murray as the founding mother. Still others would give the nod to Robert Graves, or Aleister Crowley, or Gerald Gardner. The list could be easily extended to include not only more names but whole mystical societies such as the Golden Dawn Rosicrucians or the Theosophists. Because the Craft contains a wide variety of sects (Gardnerian, Alexandrian, Georgian, Dianic), it abounds with claims and counterclaims of ritualistic authenticity, with accusations of apostacy and/or betrayal, and with endless explanations of why this or that belief or rite or tool is the key to the acquisition of enlightenment or power. One has only to glance at the opening pages of Margot Adler's definitive *Drawing Down the Moon* (1986) to get the picture. In spite of all this, I will endeavor in the next few paragraphs to hack my way through the underbrush and give the reader some idea of what probably occurred.

With the repeal of the Witchcraft Acts in Britain in 1951, the relatively small number of Frazerian and Murrayite Witches in England and North America began to come out of the closet and proselytize for the Craft. Notable among these was Gerald B. Gardner (1884–1964), a British civil servant who had immersed himself in the religious practices of the East while on duty in Malaysia and who had been converted to Witchcraft during the 1940s in England by the renown and mysterious hag, Dorothy Clutterbuck. Setting up a museum of Witchcraft on the Isle of Man in 1951 and ensconcing himself therein as the resident Witch, Gardner began to generate a good deal of newspaper publicity. He relied upon the so-called *Book of Shadows* (ostensibly a sixteenth-century guide to the Craft but in fact a homemade forgery) to offer the world a version of Witchcraft considerably different from that which appears in the work of Frazer and Murray. Adler (1986, 62) writes of it as follows:

> To Gardner, Witchcraft was a peaceful, happy nature religion. Witches met in covens, led by a priestess. They worshipped two principal deities, the god of the forests and what lies beyond, and the great Triple Goddess of fertility and rebirth. They met in the nude in a nine-foot circle and raised power from their bodies through dancing and chanting and meditative techniques. They focused primarily on the Goddess; they celebrated the eight ancient Pagan festivals of Europe and sought to attune themselves to nature.

With the publication of *Witchcraft Today* in 1954 and *The Meaning of Witchcraft* in 1959, Gardner managed not only to spark a revival of the Craft based on his own conceptions but to establish himself as a kind of guru, or founding father.

Gardner's life and work are surrounded by controversy: some regard him as a genius; others as a dangerous fraud who may have been overly fond of flagellating his female initiates (cf. Farrar 1984, 33). Still, there is no denying his influence. What is more to the point, there is no denying the spread of Witchcraft during the postwar years. By the mid-1960s, Robert Graves (1964) wrote in the *Virginia Quarterly Review* that the "old religion" was "growing fast," and that the next few decades might well witness an even more dramatic increase in both coven members and solitary practitioners. This is, of course, exactly what happened. In North America, Europe, Australia, and New Zealand, many thousands of people, from all walks of life, have discovered their way to Wicca.

The rise of the Witches has resulted from far more than the activities and writings of Gerald B. Gardner, of course. It may be attributed in large measure to the alignment of Witchcraft with such popular modern causes as feminism and the environment, to the declining family structure that we witness everywhere around us, to the advent of an increasingly impersonal technological order, and to the appearance of extraordinarily influential recent books by such authors as Margot Adler, whose work we have already cited, and Miriam Simos (or, as she modestly calls herself on her title pages, Starhawk), whose work we will take up shortly.

Witchcraft as Cult

While adherents have been gravitating to the Wiccan community in record numbers during the past two decades (in the Seattle-Vancouver area where I write there are estimated to be between six and eight thousand organized, practicing Witches), and while cultic status may eventually be shed, I believe it is fair to say that the Craft is still a cult, and I feel it will be helpful on the verge of our psychoanalysis to place it in a cultic context. This will allow us to gain a generalized picture of the movement to which we may mentally refer as we go about our examination of specific rites and tenets in subsequent sections.

The word "cult" comes from the Latin *cultus,* which signifies adoration or worship. The group, which is relatively small, offers its members a sharply defined alternative to the dominant patterns of society in the area of religious behavior. Its theological expression consists primarily of what is said and done when members gather, and this usually means the narratives, myths, and rituals that explicate the prevailing worldview. Typically, cultic theology generates statements on the ultimate nature of reality, humankind, God, and the cosmos, and it suggests that we have been tragically divorced from transcendent experience and need to refind it. Among the more recent Witchcraft groups originally inspired by Gardner and Graves, the formalism inherent in *The Book of Shadows* or *The White Goddess* has been complemented by a relaxed, participatory style that includes, along with the customary chanting and dancing, the telling of personal histories, informal group psychotherapy, the playing of spontaneous games, and general romping around.

The cult has strong, charismatic leadership (the coven priestess or priest among the Witches, for example), and is structured upon a simple, central practice that invariably commences the religious moment and that is designed to produce powerful subjective experiences in members. For adherents to the Craft, this practice consists of gathering in a circle and creating a sacred space with words, tools, and gestures. Altered states of consciousness and intense feelings of security and belonging are characteristically induced by this rite.

Separatist in nature, the cult strives to maintain strict boundaries between itself and the outside, "fallen" world. It requires not simply commitment but conformity, and often stresses its special nature through such signs as distinctive dress and diet.

It typically attracts to its ranks minorities, young people, and women—individuals who have been "put down" through discrimination and who derive a sense of equality and power from the group. Placing inner experience before outward success, the cult provides a positive, compensatory environment to many who feel a lack of personal achievement in their lives. Finally, the cult sees itself legitimated by a long tradition of wisdom and worship. The Witches like to think of their "faith" as the oldest in the world and of themselves as spiritual descendents of the Paleolithic shamans.

Methodology

With these brief historical and sociological remarks in mind we may ask, how exactly do we go about psychoanalyzing this movement with its disputations, sects, and covens scattered about the globe?

First, we study the *texts* that Witches follow in the pursuit of their religion, or, to put it another way, we analyze meticulously what might be termed the doctrinal side of the Craft. True, there is disagreement among adherents as to what is legitimate and what is not. Still, there is enough agreement among Witches on doctrinal matters for us to *easily* come away with a good psychoanalytic grasp of what is going on. Were we studying Catholicism, Buddhism, or Judaism, we would be in a position very similar to the one we are in here, and no one would suggest, of course, that Catholicism or Buddhism or Judaism are not open to psychoanalytic understanding. Moreover, because many of the symbols, rituals, and beliefs that characterize Wicca are drawn from what might be called the world's archetypal pool, we will find ourselves dealing frequently with timeless, recognizable themes that have by now become established as items for psychoanalytic inquiry. It is an aim of this book as a whole, in fact, to *use* the study of Witchcraft to shed light on other major areas of human behavior, both spiritual and secular.

Also worth underscoring is the extraordinary influence of Miriam Simos's book, *The Spiral Dance* (1979). According to Scott Cunningham (1988, 184), this text is "one of the most influential ever published on Wicca," and has had a "tremendous impact on both groups and individuals." In the view of Margot Adler (1986, 228), *The Spiral Dance* "*alone* has created a thousand women's covens and spiritual groups." Doreen Valiente (1989,

187), a friend of Gerald Gardner and a very conspicuous, influential Witch, calls Simos's volume, "practically a new *Book of Shadows*" and regards Simos herself as a kind of miraculous prophet who came along at exactly the crucial moment. "Some years ago," Valiente tells Margot Adler (1986, 86), "I did some scrying [crystal gazing] at a Sabbat, in the course of which I predicted a young priestess would arise who would do a great deal for the Craft in the future. When I read Starhawk's [Simos's] book I felt my prediction was coming true." In this way, we can rely not only upon a variety of texts which I have singled out as particularly good in revealing the essence of Witchcraft, we can also rely on a text that the Witches themselves openly regard as their latest bible. I will make very generous use of *The Spiral Dance* in the pages to follow.

The second facet of my methodology comes from the proverbial "horse's mouth," that is to say, from personal interviews which I conducted with several members of the Wiccan community, and also from my attendance at a coven meeting where I was able to participate as an observer in the activities (including the rituals) of the Craft. Let me emphasize, however, that these materials achieve their full significance *after* one has carefully studied the textual or doctrinal side of things. Indeed, it is only in the context of this book as a whole that my interviews and accounts resonate with the psychoanalytic meanings in which we are ultimately interested.

The Witches' Goal

What, then, are Witches trying to do? What is the central aim of their religion, their *faith*? From a psychoanalytic perspective, and in particular, from the perspective of the second chapter in which we viewed the child's struggle to deal with the devastating loss of fusion and omnipotence by turning to substitute objects, I would suggest that the cult of Witchcraft has been designed at the deep unconscious level to *undo* the realities that attend the passing of the symbiotic stage and the dawning of separation and smallness. To turn the same coin onto its other side, I would suggest that the cult of Withcraft has been designed to *restore* the past in a fantastic, wish-fulfilling, idealized form that reunites the practitioner with the symbiotic object and with the omnipotence and narcissism which accompany the before-separation interplay. Witchcraft aims to stand reality on its head, and by doing so, to erase the early traumas we are all obliged to experience.

As we shall see, Witches constantly perform rites in pursuit of fusion (with the Goddess) and power (of the Goddess). This expresses, quite simply and straightforwardly, their obsessive, ongoing need to deny their separation and smallness. Moreover, because separation from the caretaker is linked unconsciously with death, the seeking after the Goddess also expresses the Witch's longing for immortality. Through her/his participation in the Craft, the Witch declares at the emotive, wish-fulfilling level, "I am joined to the maternal body and am therefore omnipotent. I am not separate, I am not small. I can undo the past as it took shape in my life. I can make the world conform to my will. I do not have to accept my fantasies and imaginings as fantasies and imaginings. I can regard them as reality. I am in control—of life, death, other people, everything." If we could somehow listen to the inner world of the Witch, we would hear these themes repeated in a variety of forms over and over again.

The Persian poet Omar Khayyám wrote,

> Ah, Love, could you and I with Him conspire
> To grasp this sorry scheme of things entire,
> Would we not shatter it to bits—and then
> Remold it nearer to the Heart's Desire?
>
> (*Rubáiyát*, Stanza 99)

This is precisely what the Witch wants to do. The "scheme of things" is "sorry" because it entails separation, smallness, and death. The Witch purports through her rituals to "conspire" with the Divine and thereby to turn "things" around. She "shatters" reality "to bits," which means that she *undoes* separation and smallness (the "sorry scheme"), and she then "remolds" it in accordance with her "heart's desire," namely, her wish for eternal union and unlimited power and control. In the most general psychoanalytic sense, this is the system.

The Witches' Method

The next question must be, of course, how do Witches bring all this about? How do they undo those developmental realities that we discovered in Mahler and that comprise the very scaffolding on which our characters are built? What is their method for achieving such a colossal purpose? The answer emerges immediately, and there is only one answer: magic.

In the realm of the Witches, magic reigns supreme. It resides at the core of virtually everything they say and do. In Scott Cunningham's words (1988, 158), "Witchcraft today *is* magic," and Cunningham goes on helpfully to define magic for us as "the constructive use of little-understood forces." According to Simos's *Spiral Dance* (1979, 7), the current bible of the Craft, the life of the Witch is "infused with magic," with the "power" to "shape the unseen into form." Moreover, it is "magic" explicitly that brings about the major aim and accomplishment of the practitioner, namely, "union with the divine," with the "force that shapes reality," with the "Goddess and the God" (13–14). Let us look briefly at what psychoanalytic investigators have had to say about the nature and function of magic.

Malinowski (1925) pointed out more than half a century ago that magical acts, one and all, are "expressions of emotion," and more particularly, emotion bound up with the possession or the lack of power. Engaged in a series of practical actions, an individual often comes to what Malinowski calls "a gap" (242). The hunter loses his quarry, the sailor his breeze, the warrior his spear, or his strength. What does an individual do in such a case, "setting aside all magic and ritual"? Whether he is savage or civilized, in possession of magic or without it, his "nervous system and his whole organism drive him to some substitute activity." He is possessed by his idea of the desired end; he sees it and feels it. Hence, his "organism reproduces the acts suggested by the anticipations of hope." The individual who is swayed by "impotent fury" clenches his fists or imagines an attack upon his enemy. The lover who aches for the unattainable object sees her in visions or mentally addresses her. The disappointed hunter imagines the prey in his trap. Such behaviors are natural responses to frustrating situations and are based on "a universal psycho-physiological mechanism" (242). They engender "extended expressions of emotion in act or word" which allow the individual to "forecast the images of the wished-for results," and by doing that, to regain equilibrium and harmony with life. Thus a "strong emotional experience which spends itself in a . . . subjective flow of images, words, or gestures" leaves a "very deep conviction of its reality." To the "primitive man," or to the "credulous and untutored" of all ages, the spontaneous spell or rite or belief, with its power "born of mental obsession," must appear as a "direct revelation" from an external, impersonal force.

Now, when one compares this "spontaneous ritual and verbiage of overflowing passion or desire" with "traditionally fixed magical ritual," one cannot but note a "striking resemblance." The two "products" are "not independent of each other" (243). Magical rituals "have been revealed to man" in those "passionate experiences which assail him in the impasses of his instinctive life and of his practical pursuits, in those gaps and breaches left in the ever-imperfect wall of culture which he erects between himself and the ... temptations and dangers of his destiny" (244). We must recognize "in this," writes Malinowski, "the very fountainhead of magical belief." Magic does not come "from the air" but from "experiences actually lived through." As for magic's *persistence,* its ability to survive failure and disappointment, it comes from the fact that positive cases always overshadow negative ones ("one gain easily outweighs several losses"). Also, those who espouse and practice magic, at least in "savage societies," are individuals of "great energy" and "outstanding personality," that is to say, individuals who are capable of swaying others to their view. In every "savage society" stories of a "big magician's wonderful cures or kills" form the "backbone of belief" and contribute to the pool of living "myth" which gives the authority of tradition to current formulas and rites.

To these hugely helpful and insightful remarks I would immediately add the following: The magical rites and practices of modern Witchcraft, with their consuming interest in fusion and omnipotence, also derive from "experience actually lived through," also address "a gap," or "impasse of instinctive life." I am referring, of course, to the primal, traumatic experience of disruption that attends the passing of the symbiotic stage, that brings with it feelings of separation and smallness, and that reverberates powerfully and painfully in the psyche of many individuals for ever after, as Mahler suggested. Certainly modern Witches often address the kind of "gap" Malinowski has in mind here—the practical problem in search of a practical solution, but their deepest unconscious aim (and the foundational goal of their theology) is to close what we can think of as *the* gap, the big, lifelong one that opens as the child loses the symbiotic mother, leaves the symbiotic orbit, and confronts for the first time his existence as a small, separate creature in the world. I believe it may be said with impunity that the "magic" of *all* religion, and not only the Wiccan faith, aims to provide human beings with a solution to, or a way out of, this fundamental and ubiquitous existential dilemma.

Roheim (1955) was among the first psychoanalysts to spy the connection between magic and the traumas of the early period, and like Malinowski, he drew upon his anthropological work in making his observations. "Magic must be rooted in the child-mother situation," he writes, "because in the beginning the environment simply means the mother. Therefore, wishing or manifesting the wish is the proper way to deal with the environment" (11). Roheim then goes on to say—and let us keep our eyes open for the "gap" we found in Malinowski—"the mother is not only known by the fact that she gratifies the wishes of the child. In truth, she would never be discovered were it not for the fact that there is a gap between desire and fulfillment." More specifically, "magic originates from the child's crying when he is abandoned and angry; it is not merely the expression of what actually takes place in the dual-unity situation, but is also a *withdrawal of attachment from the object to the means by which the object is wooed,* that is, from the mother to the word and back again to the mother" (12; my emphasis). Thus it is "obvious," asserts Roheim (44), "that we grow up via magic." We "pass through the pregenital to the genital phases of organization, and concurrently our mastery of our own body and of the environment increases. This is our own 'magic,' and it is analogous in some ways to the invocation of his own 'luonto' (or nature) by the Finnish wizard" (44). In a series of key, summarizing sentences, Roheim states that "magic" is our "great reservoir of strength against frustration and defeat. Our first response to the frustrations of reality is magic, and without this belief in our own specific ability or magic, we cannot hold our own against the environment." The baby "does not know the limits of its power. It learns in time to recognize the parents as those who determine its fate, but in magic it denies this dependency. The ultimate denial of dependency comes from the all-powerful sorcerer who acts out the role which he once attributed to the projected images." While the "magical omnipotence fantasy of the child is a part of growing up, *magic in the hands of an adult means a regression to an infantile fantasy*" (45–46; my emphasis). Magic says, in the end, I refuse to give up my desires.

There is a sharp qualitative difference, then, between the kind of "magic" we use naturally during the course of our everyday lives and the kind that marks a regression to infancy. The first is rooted in what Mahler (1975, 71) calls "sound secondary narcissism," or the realistic pride we take in our accomplishments at all ages. It is rooted also in the supportive feelings that are directed toward us by other people, including, of course, the parents. This is the "magic" we associate with a "positive attitude," with a healthy confidence, and above all, with an ability to "bounce back" and "carry on" when things go badly. The second kind of magic is rooted in the "primary narcissism" of the symbiotic stage, in what might be thought of as a primitive identification with parental omnipotence. We associate it not with everyday confidence and resiliency but, as Roheim suggests, with grandiosity, with claims of supernatural power or divine gifts. One thinks here not only of the "sorcerer" Roheim mentions but of the dictator, the guru, and certain film stars as well. This basic distinction will help us to place Witchcraft, along with various other cultural activities such as economics, science, and politics, on a continuum of magical thinking.

The Magical System of Modern Witchcraft

At the center of the system stands the Goddess. As Miriam Simos (1988, xxvi) has it, connection with the Goddess *is* Witchcraft. Earlier we cited Cunningham's (1988, 158) comment that Witchcraft *is* magic. There is no contradiction here. Indeed, there is revelation. The inextricable link between the Goddess and Wiccan magical practices is a derivative of the link between the mother and infantile fantasies, as explicated in Roheim. While it is true that Witches routinely announce the importance of the God in their scheme of things, even claiming an equality between the God and his female counterpart, it is impossible to read the texts of the Craft, or to talk with Witches, or to attend coven meetings without realizing the God's predominantly formal or doctrinal significance. When one comes right down to what Witches read and say and do, it is the Goddess, not the God, who is central. However, I do not mean to exclude Him from the analysis and will bring Him in at the appropriate place.

The Goddess of the Witches is a version of the omnipotent mother as she is perceived by the infant during the symbiotic stage. She is limitless, ubiquitous, all-encompassing, all-enveloping, all-controlling. She is also the source of everything. As the old expression has it, the Goddess is the be-all and the end-all of the world. Roheim, you will recall, stated that the mother is the first environment. In Witchcraft this is explicitly pronounced in a way that focuses unforgettably not merely the aims of the early period but the manner in which those aims persistently find their way to the surface in the later worship of a substitute object.

As I earlier suggested and must reemphasize here, the core wish is to *overcome differentiation,* the stage in Mahler where fusion and omnipotence are *lost.* To overcome differentiation is to regain union, to deny separation, and to recapture omnipotence. Differentiation is the enemy to be wiped out by magic. According to Simos (1979, 8), "the Goddess is not separate from the world"; She is not *in* "reality," or a part of "reality"; the Goddess "*is* reality, *is* the world, and all things in it," including "woman and man." Becoming a Witch is a matter of "relinking" with Her endless "manifestations" (9). Simos asserts in a striking phrase that has become a canonical feature of modern Witchcraft, "one thing becomes another in the Mother" (9). Thus the Goddess, the mythic Great Mother, is ultimately and explicitly the great source of nondifferentiation, the great abolisher of boundaries, and the great blender of beings. Through Her we can collapse precisely that separateness which was accomplished with such agony during the early years and which has streaked our lives with painful undercurrents and with a continuous search for fusion through substitute objects.

Let me offer a few more examples of this theme from Simos's *Spiral Dance.* The Goddess "dissolves separation" and "glues the world together" through Her "love" (25). Each of us is "the Goddess' child, the Goddess' beloved, the Goddess' self" (15). There is no deity who stands apart from the world, an object of fear, for the world is the Goddess whose "laughter bubbles and courses through all things" (14). She manifests herself in "ordinary tasks"; no matter what you are doing, in the kitchen, in the yard, at the store, She is with you (62). Each stage of life is an aspect of Her nature; She is the moon waxing as life grows, the moon waning as life fades; She is the end of life, the way to reincarnation (65). The rain is Her "menstrual blood" (26); the "earth" is Her "body" (57). The rivers and oceans are Her "overflowing breast milk" (64). You are "one drop," Simos instructs us, in the "primal ocean" which is Her "womb." When you worship the Goddess, you "merge" with all that is of the earth: grass, fruits, beasts, stones (64). Your very susceptibility to gravity is a pull to Her bosom (64). When you breathe, it is Her breath that you take in. When you step in the oozing "mud," it is Her body that you feel (64). The four seasons are aspects and expressions of Her being. She is the "wheel of the year" (169), the "vaginal passage of rebirth" (82). As you worship Her—and here is the key metaphor—"the drought of separation is over" (71).

But it is not only the planet earth that Simos transforms into a version of the Goddess; the whole universe becomes the Great Mother. The "cosmos is modeled on the female body" (85), she writes, blithely projecting away, and everything in the cosmos, including you and me, is "charged" with the Goddess' "power." Accordingly, the most important contribution of Witchcraft to our "spiritual" perception derives from its capacity to make us see that "all is one," that the Goddess is our "cup," our "wine of life," and that She has "never been separate from us" (196–99).

Again and again, in reading texts of the Craft, one comes upon similar notions. It is a veritable endless flood. "All things come to fruition through the Goddess," writes Cunningham (1988, 71). She is "the earth, the sea, the moon, the stars," and we are part of her endless domain, joined to her "creation."

The "primordial Mother" was "bequeathed to us before the dawn of time" [that is, before the dawn of the ego, or the end of the autistic stage], declares Warren-Clarke (1987, 3). She "answers our cries," and "acknowledges Her children." We "fuse" with Her and "are one" with Her. She is the "corn, the oceans, the dew, the rivers. . . . All things are in Her, and we are in Her too" (ibid.).

"She is the Great Mother of All," states Gerald Gardner (1959, 132). All life comes from Her, and all people and things are Her "children." What are her gifts? "Magic and inspiration . . . She is the Goddess of Magic and Magicians" (133).

The Goddess is "continuous with the heavens," writes Farrar (1984, 37). She is the "giver of life," the "Mother of all creation," and the Witch is "her secret child" (20). She is "in all women" and "all women are in Her" (75). She exists now, and She existed "before the earth was formed" (100). She is "the sea, the tides, the earth, the heavens," the "Mighty One" who "governs all" (199). Farrar then goes on to state in a fascinating expression that each individual is a "part" of the Goddess' "central nervous system" (269), a part of her *body*. Underscoring this notion in another place, Farrar (1987, 3) writes that the "cosmos" is an "organism," namely, the body of the Great Goddess, and that we, as human beings, comprise that organism's "individual cells." Clearly, to discover the Goddess is to rediscover dual-unity.[1]

Magic at Work

Wiccan ceremonies invariably commence with what practitioners call "casting the circle." Here is the way it goes (in abbreviated form) in Simos (1979, 55–57):

> The room is lit by flickering candles. . . . The coveners stand in a circle. . . . The High Priestess, her consecrated knife [athame] unsheathed, steps to the altar and salutes the sky. . . . Raising her knife the High Priestess calls out, "Hail, Guardians of the Watchtowers of the East. . . . Come! By the air that is Her breath, send forth your light." . . . The High Priestess, knife held outward, traces the boundaries of the circle, and cries, "Lady of the Outer Darkness, come! By the earth that is Her body, send forth your strength, be here now!" The High Priestess traces the last link of the circle and says, "We are between the worlds." . . . The ritual is begun.

Although Simos, "for literary convenience," has the High Priestess casting the circle, "any qualified covener, female or male, may take her role" (55). Too, a solitary practitioner may commence his/her magical activities by casting a circle in the privacy of his/her own room.

Having created a sacred space and positioned herself "between the worlds," the Witch proceeds to "grounding and centering." According to Simos (1979, 49; my emphasis), this is a "basic technique of magical work" and consists of "establishing an energy connection with the earth" by "visualizing a *cord* extending from the base of your spine to the center of the earth" and by "aligning your body along its center of gravity." The Witch then "breathes from her center," from her "abdomen," and "feels the energy flowing up from the earth to fill her." Grounding is "important," writes Simos (49), "because it allows you to draw on the earth's vitality rather than depleting your own." What is the psychoanalytic significance of all this?

The circle is cast to facilitate the accomplishment of various magical ends: consecrating a tool, initiating a new member of the coven, protecting one's home and family from enemies, healing a sick friend, and so on. We must note immediately, however, that none of these ends can be achieved without *power*, the power to influence, indeed, to alter reality. "The main function of a circle," writes Farrar (1984, 82), is not "protection." It is "to preserve and contain the power that is raised within it—in other words, to concentrate and amplify the psychic efforts of the group." We must also note here the endlessly repeated Wiccan tenet that the earth is the body of the living Goddess, the Great Mother, a huge, female organism with both a "nervous system" and "awareness" (Farrar 1987, 16). In this way, power is raised in the circle by establishing a psychic link between the Witch's imaginary "cord" and an "earth" that is explicitly regarded in Craft theology as the Great Mother's living, breathing *body*.

There is an integral psychoanalytic connection, then, between the raising of power to do magic and "relinking" with the Goddess in the circle. Just as omnipotence, or power, was taken by the child from the symbiotic body of the mother during the early period, so is it now taken again from the sacred space where the Witch bonds psychically with the all-powerful Goddess. Earlier we noted Cunningham's definition of Witchcraft as "magic," along with Simos's definition of Witchcraft as "relinking with the Goddess." We now see the full unconscious meaning of this relation. Having regained fusion through the circle, the Witch immediately regains omnipotence too. They go together automatically as what we might call psychic epiphenomena. Thinking back momentarily on the work of Roheim and Malinowski, we would suggest that the Witch has attained the dual-unity Roheim spied as magic's chief end and is therefore in a mental-emotive position to accomplish those mundane purposes Malinowski singled out as magic's goal. With the power of the Goddess in hand (or, as we shall see, in wand), the Witch can remold the world closer to her heart's desire.

Circles of Power

The main function of the circle, we discovered in Farrar (1984, 82), is to raise, and to contain, power. Note the extent to which this idea is echoed and amplified in the texts of the Craft. As we gather in the cricle, join hands and breathe together, writes Simos (1979, 43), we "suck in the power" as if "through a straw." Becoming "one, one circle, one breathing, living organism," we "breathe the breath of the belly, the breath of the womb," and are "revitalized" and "renewed" through our bond to the "earth" (44–45). The circle is our "place of power," our "reservoir of power" (58, 150), and its center is our "point of transformation" (67). The circle is not "cast" to keep out "demons," writes Gardner (1988, 25), but to keep in "power." It is the "domain of the gods," of expanding "energy" and "will." It is the palce to which we are "summoned" to hear "mighty words." According to Cunningham (1988, 103–4), the circle is the "sphere of energy," the "temple of magical energy," the "powerful construction of energy." It opens us to the world of transforming ritual, and the casting of its "precedes nearly every [magical] rite." Warren-Clarke (1987, 20) suggests that we envision the circle as a "fruit" and then, in our minds, "chew on it for power." In the view of Margot Adler (1986, 109), the circle is "the container of raised energy," a "sacred space" where "contact with the gods is possible." Indeed, says Adler, when a Witch is in the circle, she/he may *become* the God or Goddess, the "archetypal force" itself.

All of this allows us to make psychoanalytic headway in grasping the manner in which energy or power is characterized by Witches in their depictions of the universe. "Energy flows in spirals," declares Simos (1979, 130); its motion is always "circular, cyclical." The universe does not simply "move," it "dances," and as it does so it creates a "swirl of energy" (1979, 20), a "spiral dance" which is *itself* the manifest Goddess releasing her power into the cosmos (1979, 14). Accordingly, the Goddess is both the galaxy in the heavens (spiral nebula, etc.), and the cycle of the seasons on the earth, the "wheel of the year" (1979, 169), winter, spring, summer, autumn. "The wheel turns," writes Simos; "on and on" it goes in its never-ending spiral expressions. From this perspective, the Witches' circle itself becomes a "living" entity, a "living mandala" (58), and not merely a line on the ground.

Farrar (1984, 83) underscores this last notion when she reminds us that casting the circle is merely putting a trace around what is actually a *sphere,* a sphere that is full of pulsating energy, a kind of "glowing, transparent, electrical globe," or ball (84). This living, vibrating entity does not only give us power; it gives us protection, too. We can "zip ourselves up in it" when we feel threatened by a "psychic attack from the outside" (84). In fact, maintains Farrar (ibid.), we do not even have to "cast a circle" on the ground if and when we wish to "zip up"; we can simply do it "mentally, often without giving any outward sign that we are doing so." Can there be any doubt at this juncture that the circle, which is the dancing galaxy, is also the protective womb, *that* glowing, vibrating *sphere?*

Power is circular in Witchcraft because the circle, in all its manifestations as symbol and coven group, is psychically bound up with the mother as both symbiotic and transitional object. It makes no difference at which conscious level the projection is operating—from the cosmos, to the earth, to the group, to the womb—the obsessive need to undo the traumas of the early period, to terminate separation and smallness, to recapture symbiosis and omnipotence, makes the unconscious tie between fusion and power automatic and inextricable, exactly as it was in the beginning, and exactly as it began to be wished-for when separation, with all its transitional agonies and longings, got underway. To maintain with the Witches that the circle's main function is to raise and contain power is affectively equivalent to maintaining that power is circular. Each notion is simply a version of the mother's body, the glowing, vibrating entity from which the practitioner was cut off at the onset of differentiation. Thus to "zip up" in the circle, either mentally or in the coven group, is to use the symbolic realm, or culture, as a substitute for the original source of narcissistic supplies and protection. It is to go back inside the omnipotent object of life's first years.

With this in mind, we will not have any trouble understanding the psychoanalytic significance of what the Witches regard as their most coveted and highest accomplishment, namely, "ruling the circle." According to Farrar (1984, 19), when a Witch has been fully initiated into the "secrets" of the Craft, when she/he has been "consecrated" and made a "priestess of the Art," a sword or "athame" is placed into her hands with the words, "now thou art ruler of the circle." When we recall that the circle is the body of the mother (Goddess), the place of fusion, power, and magical achievements, we begin to spy the very essence of Witchcraft today: It strives to control the object of the early period and by doing that to reverse the course of development during which such control was lost. To become a Witch-Priestess and thereby to "rule the circle" is to be in a psychic-emotive position to do whatever one wishes with the mother's body. One can fuse with it, zip up in it, suck its power up through one's "cord," and use that power magically to fulfill one's desires. What more can magic do? What more could one want from a cult? Surely we comprehend now the meaning of Simos's statement (1979, 2, 9), common to Witchcraft, "*you* are the Goddess; . . . *you* are divine."[2]

I suspect we also comprehend now the meaning of Simos's words (1979, 55), equally common to Witchcraft, that the practitioner, after "casting the circle," exists "between the worlds." We have, on the one hand, the world of ordinary reality, ordinary consciousness, *ordinary autonomy*—the world in which we confront, and live with, the facts of our separation and smallness, our differentiation from the environment and in particular the caretaker, our limitations as people, our mortality. We can think of this as the after-separation world, or the world that emerges after the struggle toward individuation and object constancy has occurred. On the other hand, we have the before-separation world, the world of fusion and omnipotence, of dual-unity and magical-autistic thinking, the world from which the child is torn as the drive for separation and the demands of the environment make themselves powerfully known. This is the world in which "one thing becomes another in the mother" (Simos 1979, 9), and the goal of Witchcraft, to express it from still another angle, is to cross psychological boundaries and get these worlds together so that the emotional features of the be-fore-separation world can be worked back into the after-separation world. As Simos (1979, 57) declares, "in Witchcraft, we define a new space and a new time whenever we cast a circle." In other words, "in Witchcraft" we undo precisely those perceptual categories (space and time) that are established, or fixed, as the child moves toward differentiation and the attainment of an in-dividuated ego. There is nothing "new," ultimately, about the space and time Simos refers to; we knew them before, during infancy, as paradisal merger and eternal bliss. It is an *old* story.

Patriarchal Concerns

Witches constantly pronounce their purpose of defeating the old, patriarchal "values" of terminating the aggressive, ex-ploitative era of masculine domination and war, and of restoring the mother and the Goddess to their rightful place at the center of society and the world. "Since the decline of the Goddess religions," writes Simos (1979, 8), a "male God" has "ruled the cosmos from the outside" and "shaped our perceptions uncon-sciously." Because of this, we passively accept not only the "op-pression of women" but a host of damaging "cultural pressures" that lead to "self-hatred," aggression, and the "plundering of the earth" rather than to "nurturance" and "creativity." According to Warren-Clarke (1987, 66), "an overpowering masculine force" has dominated the West for nearly three thousand years. "Ideol-ogy" has become "patriarchal and male," and this has "tipped the balance to the side of war, greed, ownership, bigotry, anger, power for power's sake, and the subjugation of women." A return to the Goddess will restore the balance and lead to "compassion, freedom, love, and wisdom." But with the context of this study firmly in mind, we immediately recognize such ideological pronouncements for what they are, namely, rationalizations for the unconscious, regressive need to get back to the mother, to restore the before-separation world with its delicious fusion and omnipotence—in a word, to get rid of the gap that yawned when symbiosis came to an end. After all, can a "religion" that encourages again and again, in a thousand glowing, passionate metaphors, the dissolving of the practitioner into the huge, breasty body of the Great Mother, that presents a view of the universe in which the individual human being comprises but a cell in the *corpus maternus*—can such a religion actually expect one to believe that it seeks to place the Goddess at the center of the world for ideological and ethical reasons?

I am not denying, of course, that Witches can have ideological and ethical concerns, nor am I denying that these may play a role in the activities and beliefs of the Craft. I am denying only that they are paramount, or exclusive. In other words, I am suggesting that the ideology sits, as it were, on top of the basic, underlying needs and wishes, concealing them in a cloud of rationalizations and noble, humanistic purposes. Patriarchy is the enemy of the Witches because patriarchy speaks for separation, for loss of fusion and omnipotence, for the individuated world of the father that succeeds the symbiotic world of the maternal figure. Witches pine nostalgically for the putative matriarchate of old because matriarchy means mother, and mother means, at the deep, regressive level, the restoration of merger, power, and bliss. Unless Witches *see* this, unless they acknowledge honestly their unconscious agenda, they will have no chance whatever of achieving maturity as human beings.

This all-pervasive longing for the maternal figure explains the persistent tendency of Wiccan texts to play up, or highlight, the benign, loving aspects of the Goddess and to play down, or soften, Her negative, harrowing features. If fusion with the Goddess is the aim of practitioners, She must be presented in a way that will encourage them to fuse with her. To express the matter in psychoanalytic terms, we would say that Witchcraft endeavors to collapse the splitting that transpires during the early period, to get rid of (deny) the "bad object," the side of the mother that enforces separation, terminates dual-unity, ends symbiosis and omnipotence. The Goddess "swells with love" for Her children and Her world, writes Simos (1979, 26). Because Her "law is love," namely, the "protective love of mother for child" (83), we may "invoke" Her "in perfect trust" (75). The Goddess' love for us is "constant, unchanging, unconditional," Simos continues

(84, 138), employing precisely those descriptive terms that characterize the perfect, idealized caretaker.

She is the "gracious, blessed Mother of all things," declares Cunningham (1988, 71), our "refuge" and our "healing." In the expression of Warren-Clarke (1987, 135), we "walk in peace upon the breast of our Earth Mother." Everything that happens to us, claims Gardner (1959, 132), is ultimately attributable to the Goddess, yet She always proceeds "in a sweetly loving way." She is the "mother who lovingly spanks and kisses her children" (ibid.). Even the Goddess as Crone, Old Age, Winter, Death is presented in these texts in a manner that denies finality, "softens the blow," makes the reality (the "spanking") a desirable, supportive one, for Winter always leads here to spring, and death always leads to rebirth. "Worship Me as the Crone," writes Cunnigham (1988, 71; my emphasis), "tender of the *unbroken cycle of death and rebirth.*" To "die" is to be "reborn" writes Simos (1979, 170), who, like Witches generally (cf. Farrar 1984, 115), expresses a belief in reincarnation in her works. To "behold the circle of rebirth," or the "cord of life" correctly is to realize that "you will never fade away" (180). As we noted earlier, the fear of death is unconsciously associated with separation from the caretaker; the Witches work hard to mold *their* Caretaker in a way that will diminish this fear.

We are in a good position, now, to grasp the principal difference between the kind of Witchcraft we encountered in Chapter 1 among the Navahó and Normanby Islanders,[3] and the kind we encounter among the modern Wiccan communites of the West. The first is largely a matter of projective expressions based on the internalization of the *bad object*. It has aggressive, manipulative ends rooted in envy, grandiosity, and the lust for power. Although our modern Witches certainly have their share of envy, grandiosity, and power-seeking, the Craft is largely a matter of projections based on the *good object*. It seeks the good breast of the mythic Goddess and strives to *deny*, rather than to actualize, the aims and affects associated with the aggressive, frustrating, and rejective side of the maternal image. Of course, like all generalizations, this one probably needs to be qualified somewhat more than I have qualified it here. Yet it is fundamentally sound, and enormously helpful in placing Wiccans among the world's practitioners of Witchery. Indeed, the emphasis on the good as opposed to the bad object characterizes the major difference between what we commonly think of as white and black magic. Members of the Wiccan community stress repeatedly that the

Witch is permitted to accomplish whatever she wishes through magic as long as she "harms none" (Cunningham 1988, 40).

We are also in a good position now to understand the role of the God in modern Witchcraft. Simos (1979, 26) writes in one place, "the view of the All as an energy field polarized by two great forces, Female and Male, Goddess and God, which in their ultimate being are aspects of each other, is common to almost all traditions of the Craft." As I suggested earlier, this is the official line: Goddess and God are equal and inextricably joined together as they manifest themselves in the world around us. However, as I also suggested, such formal, doctrinal equality is belied at the level of practice. When we come right down to what Witches do and say, we recognize at once that this is a Goddess-centered (or mother-centered) cult in which the God plays a fascinating but decidedly subordinate role. The following passage by Farrar (1984, 169; my emphasis) summarizes the matter for us as well as we could wish: "Wicca is matriarchal, and the High Priestess is the leader of the coven—with the High Priest as her partner. They are essential to each other, and ultimately equal (remembering that the immortal Individuality, the reincarnating monad, is hermaphroditic), but in the context of Wiccan working and of their present incarnation, *he is rather like the Prince Consort of a reigning Queen. He is a channel for the God aspect,* and there is nothing inferior about that; but Wiccan working is primarily concerned with the gifts of the Goddess." To capture the psychoanalytic meaning of this we must move momentarily to the oedipal level of analysis.

Modern Witchcraft reconstitutes the oedipal situation in a manner that prevents the paternal figure from impeding the mother's "gifts" of fusion and omnipotence. To be sure, the Father-God is there, and his presence allows the practitioner to participate, along with his coven siblings, in an ideal (or better, idealized) family gathering. In an age when intact, traditional families are crumbling all around us, the attraction of such an opportunity is not to be underestimated: here is the great male God, the handsome Prince Consort, and here is His wonderful Queen. "Come," says Wicca, "join the family circle and relive your oedipal journey in perfect safety and security. Was there danger and disappointment in your oedipal past? Well, erase them now. Make the world conform to your oedipal, as well as to your pre-oedipal, wishes." The Father-God's presence may also provide the practitioner with an opportunity to resist psychologically too complete, too total an engulfment into the mother's sphere. Obviously such attractions and fears will vary from one adherent to another. But what Wiccan ritual and text disclose at the bedrock is a wish to remove the Father from the center of the picture, to "take care of him" in a way that permits the Witch to stay with, and in, the *corpus maternus.* For we must remember, it is fusion with the Mother-Goddess that returns the Witch to the symbiotic stage and thus provides her with the power (omnipotence) to perform the *magic* in which her vocation is rooted.

Offering us a typical Wiccan creation myth, Simos (1979, 17; my emphasis) declares, "Alone, awesome, complete within Herself, the Goddess . . . floated in the abyss of the outer darkness before the beginning of all things. . . . The Goddess became filled with love . . . and gave birth to a rain of bright spirits that filled the world and became all things. . . . As She moved out from the Goddess, She became more masculine. First she became the Blue God, . . . then she became the Green One, vine covered. . . . At last she became the Horned God, the Hunter whose face is the ruddy sun and yet dark as death. But always desire draws Him back toward the Goddess, so that *he circles her eternally.*" Here, then, is the heart of the matter: In the beginning is the Mother, not the Father, and the Mother *remains at the center of the magic circle* with the male figure *revolving around her forever,* like a planet orbiting a sun. In *this* oedipal universe, it is the "awesome Queen" who reigns.

Initiation and the Meaning of Rebirth

A "normal Gardnerian" initiation ritual includes the following, as depicted in Farrar (1984, 10): The candidate is carried "bound and naked in torchlight procession into a cave by a group of naked women" who withdraw and "leave her terrified in pitch darkness." She gradually "conquers her fear and becomes calm," at which point the women return. They "stand in line with their legs astride," and the candidate is "ordered to struggle, bound as she is, through the vagina-like tunnel of legs," while the women "sway, howl, and scream as though in childbirth." When she is "through," she is "pulled to her feet and her bonds are cut away." The Leader then faces the candidate and offers the latter "her breasts." This "symbolises that she would suckle the candidate as she would her own child." As for the "cutting of the bonds," it "symbolises the cutting of the umbilical cord." Finally, the candidate "kisses the proffered breasts, is sprinkled with water, and told that she has been reborn into the priesthood of Moon Mysteries."

In Simos (1979, 161), one of several descriptions of initiation rituals begins with a "death cycle," an "enacted dissolution" or "symbolic annihilation and purification." Taken to an ocean beach or lakeside, the blindfolded candidate is told to "walk trustingly into the waves" where, eventually, "protective hands will pull her back" and guide her to a nearby "tub" around which a "circle is cast." Helped into the water, the candidate is "washed and chanted over by other coveners. . . . She is told to meditate, purify herself, and look for a new name." After being dried, and having one of her ankles bound with a "cord" by a Priestess, the candidate kneels in the center of the circle, vows loyalty to the Craft "on her mother's womb," and undergoes a "cutting of the cord." With this, "coven members grab her, lift her up, and carry her three times around the circle, laughing and shrieking."

The inclination of Wiccan texts to regard initiation as a symbolic death and rebirth is perfectly explicit: "Every initiation," writes Farrar (1984, 10), "is a symbolic death and rebirth," a preparation for a "new life." The initiate, writes Vivian Crowley (1989, 64, 69), is "like the child in the womb who has not yet been exposed to the light of day." She/he is "unborn," and her former life "but a dream." Coven members "await her entry into the circle of light." An initiation is a "symbolic death and rebirth," writes Simos (1979, 160), a "new beginning." As initiates, we "strip ourselves and go through the open door bound by cords." What is the psychoanalytic significance of all this?

The "rebirth" of the Witch is her second coming. She is permitted through magic to do everything all over again, and this time to get it *right*. Instead of losing omnipotence and fusion as she lost them during the course of her original development, the Witch attains the emotive, psychic capacity not only to *gain* them but to *retain* them forever. The old, bad "dream" of ordinary autonomy, and the old, bad reality of separation, smallness, and death are expunged as the "new beginning," complete with new umbilicus and name, gets underway. Does the Witch desire to stay fused with Mother-Goddess? Well then, she *will*. Does the Witch desire to sustain her omnipotence and her special, narcissistic identity? Well then, she *will*, for it is the Witch who is now in control, not the parent. It is her will that now governs the emotive, existential picture, or, as the religious terminology has it, the "new life."

Witches are fond of citing Aleister Crowley's famous definition of magic as "the Science and Art of causing change to occur in conformity with Will" (cf. Adler 1986, 8). We see now exactly what this means. It is not "change" in "conformity" with "will" in some *general* sense that the Witch is seeking. She does not crawl through "a vagina-like tunnel of legs" and undergo "rebirth" into a power-giving cult for *that.* The magic Witchcraft brings is precisely the magic of *reshaping one's psychosexual development,* of denying the smallness and separation that comprise one's ordinary autonomy. It is separation and smallness that do not "conform" to the Witch's "will." Indeed, the Witch's will to power is her wish to enter the powerhouse of the mother once again and to manage the controls forever. Simos (1979, 7) asserts in one place that a Witch becomes a "shaper" who "bends the unseen into form." We may translate: A Witch becomes a wisher who believes in her omnipotent ability to change her ordinary, actual development (achieved through the caretaker) into a shape more pleasing to her anxious, demanding ego. When a Witch says she has the "ability to bring about anything she wants," and that her "life holds infinite possibilities" (Gardner 1959, 37), we can be very sure of what it is she "wants": the "infinite" that she knew, and lost, during the early period of her existence.

Tools and Invocations

Having been "reborn," having regained the security and omnipotence of the idealized caretaker (the Goddess), the Witch wants to be *doing things,* wants to get on with the business of being a Witch. Hence, it is time for us to examine more closely the details of her craft: the tools she employs during the course of her rites and spells and the words she uses as she invokes the supernatural powers that are now available to her.

Among the items the Witch frequently employs may be numbered the wand, the cup, the cauldron, the cord, the pentacle (five-pointed star), and the athame (sacred knife). The psychoanalytic significance of these objects emerges readily from the literature. Simos (1979, 61) tells us that the "tools" of Witchcraft are "tangible representatives of unseen forces," and that to use them is to "augment the power of the mind." According to Farrar (1984, 41), the Witch's tools carry an "invisible and powerful spiritual charge" that may be traced to "bodies" on "other levels" of the universe and that may be tapped by the Witch during the course of her practice. In Farrar's view the "power" of the object increases as it is used.

To get the spiritual power lurking in the tool to work for her, the Witch must participate in a ceremony of consecration that entails a particular kind of *transference,* namely infusing the energy of one's body and mind into the already charged physical object. When this is done, the power of the object joins with the power of the individual to create the instrument of magical change. As Warren-Clarke (1987, 72) puts it, the "power of our will" enters the tool to "complete its charge" and to make it capable of assisting us "in directing the course of events." According to Simos (1979, 69), the "tool" becomes a viable instrument of Witchery when and only when it is "charged" with our "psychic energy" during the moment of consecration.

Here is the way it goes in Simos (1979, 63) with regard to the wand:

> Hold your wand in your strongest hand. Breathe deeply, and feel the power of Fire, of energy. Be aware of yourself as a channel of energy. You can change spirit into matter.... Feel your own power to create.... Be in touch with your *will*—your power to do what you must.... Let your will flow into your wand.

Here is the way it goes with regard to the athame, or sacred knife, used to demarcate space and draw circles:

> Hold your athame or sword in your strongest hand.... Feel the power of your mind to influence others and the strength of your responsibility not to misuse that power.... Let the power of your intelligence flow into your tool. (63)

Here is the cup:

> Hold your cup cradled in both hands. Breathe deep and feel the power of Water, of emotion.... The cup is the symbol of nurturing, the overflowing breast of the Goddess that nourishes all life.... Let the strength of your emotions flood the cup. (64)

And finally, the pentacle:

> Hold your pentacle in both hands. Breathe deep and feel the power of earth, of the body. The pentacle is your own body, four limbs and head. It is the five senses, both inner and outer.... The pentacle is

the four elements plus the fifth—essence. And it is the five stages of life, each an aspect of the Goddess. (65)

Let us recall at this point the manner in which objects are used *transitionally* as a way both toward the caretaker and away from the caretaker during the crisis of separation that follows the symbiotic stage of development. As the traumatic diminution of omnipotence and fusion takes place with the passing months and years, the child turns to substitutes—teddy bears, blankets, story books—that facilitate his transition *away* from the relationship with his mother, and that also enable him to continue *in* that very relationship at the level of fantasy and emotion. Such items (Winnicott calls them "transitional objects," as we saw in Chapter 2) attest to our distinctive, paradoxical capacity as humans to move in two opposing developmental directions at the same time. In this way, the child learns to use the objects around him in the culture to preserve his security, his tie to the maternal and/or paternal figure, while he struggles to achieve a measure of his own power, his own control.

So it is with the Witch's tools: Note that she takes them up *after she has been reborn,* after the commencement of her "new existence," her "new life," her new *bonding* with the Mother-Goddess. Just as the original transitional object recalls the mother's omnipotence, just as it must be invested projectively with qualities of the mother which the child has internalized along the way, so must the Witch complete the tool's transformation by "breathing" her "power," her "energy," into it and by uttering magical words of consecration which explicitly recall the "overflowing breasts" of "the Goddess," the "unseen force" that comes not from "other levels of the universe," but from the nursery. The magical formula for the tool's transformation is, then, perfectly obvious from a psychoanalytic perspective: After consecretion the tool is *reinternalized* to become part of the Witch's new identity, part of the new existence in which *her will,* not the parent's, controls the course of events. As a new transitional object, the tool moves the practitioner back to the Goddess and away from the Goddess in the same psychological moment. It both relinks her with the omnipotent mother and grants her fresh, autonomous power, exactly as the original objects of transition did.

What we see in regard to the pentacle is especially fascinating here, for when Simos (1979, 65) declares that the pentacle represents the body—the four limbs and the head—she reminds us of the Craft's insistence that the body of the practitioner is the Goddess and the Goddess the body of the practitioner. "She is the body," writes Simos (1979, 78), "womb, breast, belly, mouth, vagina, penis, bone, and blood. . . . Whether we are eating, sleeping, making love, or eliminating body wastes, we are manifesting the Goddess." The reborn Witch experiences not only her "tool," but her whole body as a transitional object—tied to the Great Mother and a manifestation of Her, and yet a willful, magic-working entity in its own right. Thus, in a very special psychoanalytic sense, the Witch's body itself becomes a "tool," a link to the past and a means to the attainment of omnipotence in the present and future. Can we miss, now, the significance of Farrar's (1984, 45) instruction that the Witch, to get power into the athame, "should press it against her body for a time" and thereby "impregnate" it with her "aura"? We have here the early, primitive transitional dynamics acted out all over again in symbolic disguise.

Much the same reasoning may be applied to Wiccan invocations. As the Witch takes up her consecrated wand, or cup, or pentacle, or athame, she calls upon the Goddess to come and assist her in the performance of a particular rite. Here is an example from Simos (1979, 56):

> Hail, Lady of the outer darkness!
> We invoke you;
> Center of the sky,
> Fertile field,
> Come!
> By the earth that is Her body,
> Be here now!

Or again:

> Hail guardians of the watchtower,
> Rain on us,
> Help us to remember
> The ocean womb from which we come.
> Now let all of us be connected.
> Let our moods be flowing. . . .
> Until all is one.
> Let the drought of separation be over.
> Blessed be.

(71)

And finally,

> Nameless One,
> Eternal,
> Open our hearts!
> That we may live free at last. . . .
> Mother of all life,
> Engulf us with your love,
> Breathe with our nostrils,
> Touch with our hands,
> Kiss with our lips!

(105)

As Roheim (1955, 9) reminded us earlier, "more than anything else, magic consists of incantations or of mere wishes which have been uttered. The child utters sounds and the mother reacts to the cry or the call of the babbling." And as we noted in Chapter 2 while discussing the onset of verbalization, the word serves the child as a way both toward the emerging culture and back to the maternal object during the developmental crises of separation and rapprochement. Indeed, language may well be goaded into existence by the trauma of separation, by the anxiety that arises as the mother gradually but persistently disengages herself from her offspring. In this way, the invocation or magical word is, like the magical tool, a means of relinking with the Mother-Goddess after one's "rebirth," and a means of drawing on the Mother-Goddess' energy to accomplish omnipotently one's newly discovered ends. The internalized power of the original caretaker is once again projected, but this time into an *image,* a verbal embodiment of the *corpus maternus,* as opposed to a physical item, or "tool." It is the passionately uttered *word,* the semantic equivalent of Roheim's "cry," that will make Mother-Goddess "react." It is the grown-up, syntactic "babbling" that will make her "come" and "bless" her Wiccan children.

The eager activity of the Witch, her enthusiastic employment of tools and invocations, must not prevent us from appreciating the ultimately regressive nature of her conduct. True, she moves away from the Goddess as well as toward the Goddess with her pentacles and wands and cups and magical utterances. But she moves away as a *reborn child,* as one who chooses to deny and expunge her actual birth and development, her actual separation from mother, her actual smallness and mortality. We do not have to wrack our brains to figure out who and what is behind the Witch's invocational cries, "Let separation be over"; "remember the ocean-womb from which we come"; "mother of all life, engulf us." It is not the "mother of all life" but the mother of *this life, her life,* upon whom the Witch is calling, for that is the only mother she knows, and that is the mother she unconsciously projects into her tools and her prayers. In all of this, we see the past repeating itself compulsively and obsessively, which is precisely what is wrong with this religion and perhaps with all religion: It does not truly move us forward, perceptually or intellectually or emotionally. It leaves us floundering in current versions of old issues. Like the little child of scriptural prophecy, the reborn Witch enters the kingdom of heaven through her magical endeavors, but it is a heaven of denial, a heaven of omnipotent, narcissistic wishes, a heaven in which dependency is pathetically acted out in rituals that ostensibly speak for independence and strength. Witchcraft does more than remind us of the extent to which the early period of our lives can govern or *dictate,* our present behavior; it allows us to perceive a measure of heroism in all those actual little children who underwent the developmental crises of their lives and who refused to deny reality when they grew up.

Omnipotence: The Limitless Self

Linked with the Goddess, possessed of wondrous tools and invocations, the Witch is now in a position to manifest her belief in her own omnipotence. The way this goes in the literature is unforgettable and calls to mind Malinowski's fundamental insight that magic is purely and simply an expression of emotion, a desire, a wish that something might be brought about or be otherwise than it is. "A child," writes Simos (1979, 23), who discloses more than she realizes by the analogy, "makes-believe that she is a queen; her chair becomes a throne." A Witch "makes-believe that her wand has magic power, and it becomes a channel for psychic energy." Lifting her wand into the air and invoking the Goddess (we may call this, officially, the posture of omnipotence), the Witch concentrates upon achieving a particular aim. This is termed, among Wiccans, "raising a spell," and may be regarded from a psychoanalytic point of view as a kind of projective identification or psychical transference and the modal expression of omnipotence in action. When she feels that her "spell" has been attached to the person or item upon which she has been concentrating (wand in air), the Witch completes the transferential change or alteration of the environment by saying, simply, it is so—in other words, by verbally insisting upon the efficacy of her concentration and the corresponding result.

Here is an example from Simos (1979, 122, 134). We may imagine the following words spoken as the Witch concentrates upon "healing a broken heart," helping a coven member succeed in business, "attracting love" or "money," or any such task:

> Source to source
> Flow through me. . . .
> As I will
> So shall it be.
> Spell make it so!
> (Lower hands as you
> speak until wand
> touches ground.)

Thus do we behold the omnipotence of thought in all its pathetic, naked simplicity: A person wants something, wishes for it, and believes he will get it. What was learned so deeply during the early period, namely that all one had to do to achieve one's end was *will* it and *express* it, is never forgotten. And no wonder, for how could such a marvelous situation ever be relinquished in the unconscious? As Simos (1979, 132) states, capturing for us once again the simpleminded essence of the business, Wiccan "magic teaches us" that our powers, our "energies," are "unlimited, infinite. . . . Our voices carry power, the power to create, to change the world. . . . Our voices are sacred. . . . Open your eyes and look about you. . . . Feel your strength sparkling through your body. This is power." The reborn Witch, her eyes newly "opened," feels regressively once again the emotional, bodily "sparkle" experienced by the omnipotent child in his magical fusion with the caretaker.

Is the Witch afflicted by loneliness? Well, how does she deal with this dilemma, one of the banes of human existence? She adopts the posture of omnipotence (wand raised on high), recalls her link to the Goddess, concentrates her energy into a "spell," and says, "Loneliness, be gone!" That is all there is to it. In Simos's (1979, 118) words, the Witch will now "feel free of loneliness." Does the Witch have an enemy? Well, what does she do about it? She casts a circle, takes a doll in her hand, visualizes a net falling over the doll, adopts the posture of omnipotence, and says, "So be you bound, as I desire" (Simos 1979, 126). Her enemies haven't a chance.

According to Farrar (1984, 238), the "best spells" are created by "using your own imagination and devising them." Does a friend suffer from paranoia? Well, adopt the posture of omnipotence, invoke the Goddess, and repeat the word "paranoia" over and over again. This will "build up a thought-form," or "raise a spell," which one can then "activate" and "discharge" toward the sufferer by "focusing" it into its "quasi-independent existence" (240). If all goes well, the result will be as one wishes—the paranoiac will experience a diminuition of his malaise. If we are gathered in a coven and have a magical aim, we can employ "linked-hand magic." This "limbers the psychic muscles and builds up a cone of power." When we have decided on our objective, when, in Farrar's (239) words, "our wishes have been named," we wait for the coven leader to cry, "Let go!" and then we "visualize the power flying outward to achieve its various objectives." I could cite dozens of similar examples from the Wiccan texts.

The reader may be wondering, of course, how Wiccans go about explaining such omnipotence of thought. After all, we live in an age of science, of empiricism, experimentation, and debate, and we would expect Witchcraft's appeal to the primitive unconscious to be supported by some sort of argument. As we saw in our opening chapter, the ranks of the Craft are currently filled with people from all walks of life—lawyers, doctors, engineers, nurses, cooks, couriers, and computer programmers. Surely among these motley practitioners are some who find themselves unwilling simply to take things at face value.

Wiccan texts offer the reader a continuous stream of intellectual self-justification that takes the form of metaphysical claims (by analogy and of a general nature), reminders of the mysteries of modern physics, and references to the work of C. G. Jung. "There is a power in the universe," writes Cunningham (1988, 19) in what turns out to be a typical Wiccan intellectual moment. It can be used for both good and evil, and it can also be "roused, concentrated, and programmed to effect a specific result, as in a spell." Such a process, continues Cunningham (21), "may entail creating and holding certain images and concepts in the mind." True, we cannot at present "explain how this works," but "fringe physics is coming close to this achievement" (23). I leave it to the reader to judge the value of this kind of thinking. In another of his books, Cunningham (1989, 5) informs us that "the physical world is one of many realities" (a ubiquitous cliché among Wiccans). He then proceeds to declare that "the only difference between the physical and the spiritual is that the former is denser." May I say with impunity that such a statement begs a few additional questions?

"Witches are not fools," says Farrar (1984, 105); they live in "the twentieth century, not the Middle Ages," and there are a good many "scientists and technicians" among them. The "working power of the Craft arises from the emotions, from the vasty deep of the Collective Unconscious" as described by Jung. The "Gods and Goddesses" of Witchcraft "draw their forms from the numinous Archetypes which are the mighty foundation-stones of the human racial psyche." Exactly how this occurs is never explained by Farrar, any more than it is by Gardner (1959, 43), who makes a similar claim. But then, the matter was never fully or satisfactorily explained by Jung who struggled throughout the course of his life to understand the nature of what he chose to call "archetypes."

Farrar (1984, 107) proceeds to declare that "reality exists and operates on many levels," that "each of these has its own laws," and that "these sets of laws are compatible with each other and govern the interaction between the levels." When a Witch raises and casts a spell, she has simply discovered a "point and area of interaction between the levels" (109). Magic "does not break the laws of nature"; it "obeys laws that the observer has not yet understood." Thus Witchcraft is "the philosophical framework into which every phenomenon, from chemistry to clairvoyance, from logarithms to love, can be reasonably fitted." Needless to say, it would be wonderful to behold "every phenomenon" (including spells) fitted into Witchcraft's "philosophical framework"—I mean in a detailed, specific, systematic way. But, alas, this never occurs in Farrar, or in the work of any other Witch. What we get in the end is a wide variety of unorganized, unsupported observations and general, overall claims—in other words, a farrago of pseudo-scientific and occult speculations.[4]

Psychology is simply a branch of magic, writes Simos (1979, 192), as both "psychology and magic purport to describe and change consciousness." Although Witchcraft's "testing" of magical rites to see if they work is somewhat more "subjective" than scientific procedure (is this, perchance, an understatement?), yet science and religion are ultimately on a par in that each "is a set of metaphors for a reality that can never be completely described or comprehended" (190). That many kinds of "psychology" exist, some of which are given to rigorous experimental methodology and the systematic compilation of clinical data over decades; that "science" comes by its "metaphors" in ways that are entirely different from the "testing" of Wiccan rites and spells—all this is of little concern to Simos and, apparently, her followers. Witchcraft, psychology, science—they are all essentially similar; to believe in Witchcraft, psychology, science really amounts to the same thing. There isn't much difference, ultimately, between Gerald Gardner running around the Isle of Man with his cords and wands, and Albert Einstein sitting down to his desk at Princeton.

Simos (1979, 129) writes in one place that the Witch's power to "shake the world" is "most perilous, dangerous." Hence, it must "follow knowledge," "serve need," and be employed in a "cleansing, healing" fashion. But the real danger here, I would submit, is the belief in one's omnipotence, the unwillingness to acknowledge one's limitations—in short, the refusal to grow up and join the human race. In this denial, in this infantile, narcissistic imperviousness to the facts of one's development, there resides a major threat to the welfare and advancement not only of the individual psyche but of the social realm as well: A good measure of the violence, havoc, and general suffering that people have had to endure in this world has stemmed from those grandiose characters who have regarded themselves precisely as our prophetess Simos (1979, 13) urges her followers to regard themselves, namely as "manifest gods," as "divine" and "sacred" (9). The "knowledge" that is needed here is the knowledge of the early period of existence when problems of separation, along with oedipal rivalries, awaken the taste for omnipotence and self-aggrandizement. This is the knowledge that has a "healing, cleansing" potential. The working of Wiccan spells ultimately calls to mind Harold Searles's (1984, 38) observation that disturbed individuals struggle to mature and become fully human *without* relinquishing their infantile omnipotence.

Six Wiccan Rituals

1. DRAWING DOWN THE MOON

Adler (1986, 19) calls this ritual "one of the most serious and beautiful in the modern Craft." The Priestess "invokes the Goddess or Triple Goddess, symbolized by the phases of the moon and known by a thousand names. . . . In some Craft rituals the Priestess goes into a trance and speaks; in other traditions the ritual is a more formal dramatic dialogue, often of intense beauty, in which, again, the Priestess speaks, taking the role of the Goddess. In both instances the Priestess functions as the Goddess incarnate, within the circle." Adler then describes the "feeling of power and emotion" that comes over her as she "listens to the words of the Great Mother."

In Simos (1979, 166), the rite goes (in abbreviated form) like this:

Waxing Moon Ritual
(To be performed after the first visible crescent has appeared.)
On the altar, place a bowl of seeds. Fill the central cauldron with earth, and place a candle in the center. When the coven gathers, begin with a breathing meditation. A Priestess says, "This is the time of the beginning, the seed time of creation, the awakening after sleep. Now the moon emerges, a crescent out of the dark; the Birthgiver returns from death. Tonight we are touched. . . . She changes everything She touches."

Purify, cast the circle, and invoke the Goddess and God. A covener chosen to act as Seed Priestess takes the bowl of grain from the altar, saying, "Blessed be, creature of earth, moon seed of change, bright beginning of a new circle of time. Power to start, power to grow, power to make new, be in this seed." . . . Going sunwise around the circle she offers the bowl to each person . . . Each person visualizes a clear image of what they [*sic*] want to grow. . . . One by one, they plant the seeds in the cauldron. . . . Together, they raise a cone of power to charge the seeds and earth with energy. . . . Share cakes and wine, and open the circle.

Full Moon Ritual
(To be performed on the eve of the full moon.)
The circle gathers, does a breathing meditation, and a Priestess says, "This is the time of fullness, the flood tide of power, when the Lady in full circle of brightness rides across the night sky. . . . This is the time of the bearing of fruits. . . . The Great Mother, nurturer of the world pours out her love and her gifts in abundance. . . . Purify, cast the circle and invoke the Goddess and the God. . . ." One covener moves to the center of the circle and speaks her name. The others repeat it, and chant it, raising a cone of power as they touch her, earthing it into her and filling her with the power and the light of the moon. She returns to the circle and another covener takes her place. . . . A final cone can be raised for the coven as a whole. . . . Share cakes and wine and open the circle.

Dark Moon Ritual

(To be performed on the waning moon. A crystal or scrying bowl should be placed in the center of the circle.)

Gather and meditate on a group breath. A Priestess says, "This is the ending before the beginning, the death before new life. . . . The moon is hidden, but the faintest of stars are revealed and those who have eyes to see may read the fates and know the mysteries. The Goddess, whose name cannot be spoken, naked enters the Kingdom of Death." . . . Cast the circle. . . . The Leader leads a chant:

    LEADER: "She lies under all, She covers all."

    ALL: "She lies under all, She covers all. . . ."

Continue as long as there is energy and inspriation. . . . Build into a wordless power chant. . . . Crystal gaze together, sharing what you see. Share cakes and wine, and open the circle.

Warren-Clarke (1987, 86) offers practitioners the following instructions as they perform this rite: "Extend your arms out and up, and with your Will proceed to Draw Down the Moon. Breathe deeply and visualize a stream of force entering into you from the Moon's light, the Essence of the Goddess."

Psychoanalytic Notes. This metaphor reveals the underlying purpose of the Craft as a whole. The moon is, of course, a projective version of the maternal figure, and the fantasy embedded in the rite is to pull the mother back into the psychological orbit of the individual. As we have seen, the onset of differentiation marks the loss of fusion and omnipotence. The mother moves away, into "outer space" as it were; she is no longer directly in the sphere of the child's will. Thus to "draw the moon down," to bring it back or near with one's willful effort, is to deny and to reverse the central, traumatic event of infancy and childhood. The rite expresses, on the one hand, the individual's belief in his own omnipotent capacity to undo the past, to get the mother back, and it expresses, on the other, the individual's wish and need to *have* the mother's power, that "stream of force" which "enters him" as he basks in the Moon-Goddess' "light." This is, surely, the way the child feels as he participates in the mother's omnipotence, in her magical, immaterial energy, or as Warren-Clarke puts it, her "essence."

Drawing Down the Moon also comprises a fantastic attempt to allay unconscious anxiety by mastering the maternal object in several of her "phases." These correspond, at their metaphorical core, to aspects of developmental interaction as described in Mahler and in object relations generally. When the moon is "slim," when it does not shine upon us with the radiance we require, when, in short, it metaphorically harbors a facet of the bad object, we do not have to be afraid or anxious: The mother is slowly getting full, slowly coming to birth, or seed. Soon we will have our emotional nourishment, our narcissistic supplies; soon we will be "blessedly" included in a "new circle of time." The full moon celebrates the maternal figure in her idealized form, replete with life and power. Here is the full breast, the loving, nurturing object for which the practitioner yearns most deeply, and the aim of the rite, quite simply, is to draw this down to the mouth, to get the love and the power inside. Once again in Simos's words, each covener is to be "filled with the power and the light of the moon." When the moon is absent, or "dark," when the mother is not there at all, we are also comforted, for we are told, first, that her absence is not permanent. Just as the baby-sitter reassures the child who wakes up and finds the parent gone, so does the ritual reassure the Witch. Second, and perhaps more significantly, the ritual informs the practitioner that the absent mother is actually present; although she cannot be seen, she is there: "She lies under all, and she covers all," says the Leader, and the coven members repeat the words. Here we see echoed the child's first, primitive efforts at internalization of the maternal image and the object constancy that such internalization brings. We also see echoed early efforts at specifically transitional phenomena—like the baby's blankie, the Goddess "lies under all and covers all." Finally, as coveners move to the circle's center to gaze into the crystal ball, they collectively allay anxiety about the future, the time during which the absent object is scheduled to return. Taken as a whole, Drawing Down the Moon acts out obsessively several major conflicts of the mother-child relation.

2. THE MIRROR RITUAL

In Warren-Clarke's (1987, 45) version of the ritual, one sits in front of a "fairly large mirror" and, with open eyes, "goes into meditation." Rocking back and forth and chanting his "own name," the practitioner "every now and then" interrupts the chant with the words, "I am." Warren-Clarke insists that one "does *not* lose eye contact with himself" during the course of this rite, which concludes with the words, "I am who I am and I am one." Cunningham's (1988, 55) rendition has the Witch "gazing at his reflection in the mirror" and pronouncing these words: "Love is before me, behind me, beside me, above me. . . .

Love flows from me, love comes to me, I am loved." For Cunningham, a "small mirror" that enables one to "see his face within it" is sufficient for the purpose.

Psychoanalytic Notes. We have here another striking example of modern Witchcraft's endless preoccupation with issues of separation and union, and in particular with the mirror stage of development during which the child begins to establish an identity distinct from the mother's. So persistently does the loss of symbiosis and the trauma of differentiation echo in the unconscious of the practitioner that he must act the matter out over and over again, reassuring himself that he has survived and does in fact exist. What the child apprehends as the loss of the mother during the onset of differentiation is often accompanied by feelings of rejection. Cunningham's version of the mirror ritual strives to reassure the Witch that he can still love and be loved in spite of his differentiation from the original object. The emergence of a separate identity during the mirror stage depends upon mutual face-gazing activity between mother and child. Such activity is indeed one of the earliest ego-formative interactions between humans. The Wiccan rite focuses intensely upon staring at one's own face—a new version of the old, primal relation and an attempt to transform one's countenance into a transitional object on which one can depend emotionally in the present, postmaternal environment.

3. The Openings of the Body Ritual

Described by Farrar (1984, 85) as a "time-honored method for the psychic protection of an individual," the rite can be performed "either by oneself or by one's working partner." For "obvious practical reasons," the "person to be protected" undergoes the ritual naked, or as Witches are fond of saying, "skyclad." Here are Farrar's instructions: "Moisten the index finger of the right hand with a consecrated salt-and-water mixture, and touch each of the openings of the body in turn saying each time, 'Be thou sealed against all evil.' Strongly visualize the seals which you are creating. . . . On a man: right eye, left eye, right ear, left ear, right nostril, left nostril, mouth, right nipple, left nipple, navel, tip of penis, anus. . . . On a woman [the same, with the female sexual parts indicated]." As to whether or not this ritual is preferable to the casting of a protective circle, Farrar contends that an individual who is on the move will find it particularly useful: "A cast circle *can* be carried with you as you move (we have often cast a circle round a moving car, for instance), but it requires deliberate and continuing visualization." The openings of the body ritual, by contrast, "accompanies you like a suit of armor wherever you go."

Psychoanalytic Notes. So salient is the omnipotence of thought here that it may easily obscure the ritual's transitional purpose. One wishes to be protected and one therefore indulges in simple magical thinking in order to fulfil one's wish, but underlying the wish for protection is the unwillingness to face danger (or what is perceived as danger) alone—without the protective presence of the parental figure. Naked, the practitioner returns to the early period during which the mother's omnipotence enclosed the child permanently within its protective "armor." As we earlier demonstrated, the circle in modern Witchcraft is a symbolic expression of the primary caregiver, and as Farrar's work makes clear, the openings of the body ritual is psychologically equivalent to casting a protective circle. Thus it strives omnipotently, like Drawing Down the Moon, to refind the symbiotic mother, the good object who seals one off from invasion by the "bad" or "evil" forces of the world. In most cases, of course, these forces are the projective expressions of one's own psyche (the bad object) and hence the source of obsessional conduct, such as we witness here.

4. The Circle of Stones

Used to "raise energy" for the working of magic, the rite requires, in Cunningham's (1988, 105) words, "four large flat stones" and a lengthy piece of "white or purple cord." After "cleansing the area" with a "ritual broom," one places the first stone to the North, and the second, third and fourth to the East, South, and West. "This square," says the author, "represents the physical plane on which we exist: the Earth." One then takes his length of cord and lays it out circularly around the stones. "Now you have a square and a circle, the circle representing the spiritual reality. As such, this is a squared circle—the place of interpenetration of the physical and spiritual realms." The next step is to "set up the altar" and get hold of one's "tools": wand, athame, pentacle, censer, and whatever else one requires for a particular magical purpose. When one has completed his "consecrations," he "stands facing North at the edge of the cord-marked circle and summons up his power, readying it to be projected during the circle-casting." It is through one's "visualization" that the circle is created. One "walks slowly around the circle's perimeter clockwise" with feet *inside* the cord and with one's "words and energy charging the area." Let the "power flow out of your knife's blade," instructs Cunningham, "stretch the energy out until it forms a complete sphere around the working area. . . . Then say, 'Here is the boundary of the Circle of Stones. . . . Charge this by your powers, Old Ones [a reference to the Goddess and God]'." Moving to the North, one holds his wand "aloft" [the posture of omnipotence), and says, "O Spirit of the North Stone, I call you to attend this circle." One behaves similarly at the Eastern, Western, and Southern points, until "The circle lives and breathes about you. The Spirits of the Stones are present. Feel the energies. Visualize the circle glowing and growing in power." Magic, Cunningham declares, may now be "wrought."

Psychoanalytic Notes. The purpose of this rite is to recreate and to reenter the mother's body. As we have seen, the Earth in Witchcraft represents the Great Goddess, and the stones in this ritual represent "the Earth." We do not have to struggle to grasp the underlying significance of the "cord" that surrounds the stones. Having refashioned symbolically the *corpus maternus,* and having equipped himself with magical tools, the practitioner literally steps inside the "sphere," charges it with "energy," and thus erases the primary psychological *boundary* that was established between mother and infant during the differentiation phase of development. It is not the "physical and spiritual planes" that "interpenetrate" here but the past and the present, and more specifically the before-separation and after-separation worlds. The practitioner of this ritual, like the practitioner of Drawing Down the Moon, believes that he has the power to reconnect with the omnipotent object, to rediscover the wondrous union of the early period. At the same time, he performs the rite to *gain* the omnipotence he associates with the parental presence. Wand "aloft," he calls upon the "Old Ones," the "Spirits of the Earth," to cause the circle of energy in which he stands to glow and grow in power so that his "magic" might be "wrought." To consider The Circle of Stones in its entirety is to realize that modern Witchcraft comprises a war upon human limitation. Accordingly, it attracts to its ranks individuals who simply cannot or will not relinquish an infantile demand that might be stated this way: I must be joined with my omnipotent mother forever; I must continue to possess the special, unlimited powers that I enjoyed during the initial stages of my life.

5. THE DOLL OR STUFFED ANIMAL RITUAL

After casting a circle and lighting a candle, one takes a doll or stuffed animal in his hands, sprinkles it with consecrated saltwater, and gives it a name. Then, according to Simos (1979, 121), one holds it in his arms, coos to it, rocks it, and tells it "everything one would have liked to hear" as a child. "Playing" thus, one "raises energy" through "visualization" and "pours it into the doll." This "creates an image of one's child self as one would have liked it to be." When the doll is "glowing with white light and love," the practitioner concludes the ritual by kissing it, wrapping it in a white cloth, and "laying it to rest on the altar."

Psychoanalytic Notes. Playing with substitute objects is one of the chief methods through which the child attempts to resolve the crisis of separation that confronts him/her during the early period. The doll, the blankie, the teddy moves the child *away* from the mother and toward the cultural realm at the same time that it allows him to *stay* with the mother emotionally. Psychoanalysis, following the lead of D. W. Winnicott, terms such behavior "transitional," as we noted in Chapter 2. The practitioner of this rite has failed to resolve transitional problems satisfactorily. He is therefore attempting (here is the omnipotence) to "do it all over again" *without* the separation and loss that of necessity attends the onset of differentiation. "Raising energy" through "visualization," he projects it into the substitute object which is immediately transformed into an idealized version of himself as neonate. Thus he resolves the transitional dilemma by magically becoming both mother and child at once. He is born again, named again, cooed again, and rocked again *by himself.* There is no parental figure here to push him away, to demand that he exist on his own as a separate, differentiated creature. Once again we behold modern Witchcraft's obsessional longing for the good object, for the never-never land of eternal fusion, for that place over the rainbow where we are perfectly loved, perfectly secure, all wrapped up in white and resting blissfully on the Great Mother's bosom (the altar).

6. THE GREAT RITE

This is, quite simply, sexual intercourse Wiccan style, which means sexual intercourse that is linked symbolically to the body of the Great Mother. "Sexuality," writes Simos (1979, 195), "is a manifestation of the Goddess." Indeed, "all the acts of love" *belong* to the Goddess who says "they are mine." When an individual achieves "orgasm," it is not only his own "pleasure" that he/she feels, but the "moving force" of the "Mother" as well (79). As Cunningham (1988, 131) conceives it, "sex" is a union with another person *and* with the Mother-Goddess who created us.

In the words of Farrar (1984, 32), it is the "Great Rite" that celebrates our "holy, divine" connection to the "Goddess and the God."

Psychoanalytic Notes. The appeal of all this is twofold. There is, on the one hand, the sheer titillation that derives from associating sexuality with the parent, with the forbidden, incestuous object. The "feeling of incredible erotic intensity" referred to by the Witch Alara Bretanne (1989, 10) in her review of Qualls-Corbett's *The Sacred Prostitute* comprises a good example. By relinking our sexual behavior to the "sensuality of the Goddess," writes Bretanne, we can reconnect our "passion" to the "depths of our unconscious minds" and thereby renew our "spiritual natures." Permit me to suggest that there is nothing very "spiritual" about this. Indeed, the putative "spirituality" is merely a screen behind which one's incestuous proclivities can be indulged in relative safety. Bretanne gets it right when she brings in the connection between "passion" and the "unconscious," but she gets it wrong when she tries to make the unconscious religious or spiritual. It is the familial, personal unconscious that is at work here, troublesome as that may be for the ardent practitioner. On the other hand, there is the *transitional* appeal of the "rite." I mean, by linking sexuality to the Goddess, by going to bed with our partner and the Great Mother too, we remain in the protective circle of the first relationship. Our genital behaviors harbor the soothing and reassuring overtones of the oral stage. We enjoy the kind of fusion, the kind of merging and blending of boundaries, that we associate with the early period and with the good object who resides at its center.

But Wiccan sexuality can also be put to magical purposes which allow us to behold the coital partners indulging both their sensual nature and their psychological omnipotence. A "couple" who wishes to use "sex magic" for a "worthwhile objective," writes Farrar (1984, 171), will "cast a Circle around themselves," and make "love" therein. "Building up sexual tension-in-unity to the highest possible peak ... they will aim at simultaneous orgasm, at which point they will hurl the whole power of the vortex into the achievement of their magical objective." In modern Witchcraft, then, we can "screw" our way toward the achievement of our goals. The "circle" in which we indulge ourselves is a magical provider not only of the security we seek but of the power we aspire to as well. Yet how could it be otherwise? For as we have seen repeatedly, the circle in modern Witchcraft turns out to be the body of the Great Mother herself. Reunited unconsciously with that body, we transfer our infantile omnipotence to the sphere of our sexual conduct.

Several of the rites at which we have glanced can be performed by solitary practitioners. When a rite unfolds in the context of the coven, however, it will be enhanced by the psychological dynamics peculiar to such gatherings. As members join hands around the circle, writes Simos (1979, 41–45), they feel "close," secure, bound together by their practice. They "breathe one breath" and "become one," inhaling the "odor of the womb." The coven has many significances, of course, but the foundational one is captured by Ashbach and Schermer (1987, 6) when they observe that "the group often takes on the qualities of the maternal object," and that "group fantasy and ritual are simultaneously ways in which the membership defends against primitive anxieties." Where Wiccans are concerned, such primitive anxieties have a great deal to do with separation from the caretaker and the loss of omnipotence that attends the onset of differentiation. In a fascinating phrase (slip?), Simos (1988, 134) declares that the coven comprises "one nation indivisible," thus disclosing the extent to which the group can absorb those emotions ordinarily transferred to the nation—one's "motherland," one's "fatherland," the macroscopic *home.* Finally, when a meeting has concluded and members are free "to go their separate ways," they all say together, "the circle is open but unbroken" (Simos 1979, 45). In other words, coven members are *never* obliged to be separate; they carry each other (and the Goddess) around on the inside even while they are "on their own," just as the child carries around his internalized image of the mother.

Trance and the Astral Journey

Induced through a kind of meditative visualization, trance is the extreme instance of the persistent imaging Witches do in their transitional quest to rediscover and hold on to the caretaker. Simos (1979, 144) discloses the essence of the business when she writes that "in trance we find revelation. We invoke and become Goddess and God, linked to all that is. We experience union, ecstacy, openness. The limits of our perception dissolve. . . . We dance the spiral dance of existence." Simos also observes here that trance can be "dangerous" because it "opens the gates to the unconscious mind." As we noted earlier, the "spiral dance" is one of Witchcraft's chief expressions for the ubiquitous, all-encompassing, all-powerful Goddess. Hence the appeal of trance (that it permits us to reenter the *corpus maternus*) harbors a measure of anxiety: We may regressively "dissolve" into the mother's body, become engulfed in it, as we were long ago.

The astral journey (or astral projection) commences with the practitioner casting a protective circle around himself. He then induces a trancelike state by imaging, say, the "temple of Isis" with its "great hall and pillars" (Simos 1979, 143). As the trance deepens and the "astral vision takes charge," the practitioner undergoes a "separation of his astral body from its physical housing." He then "projects" that "astral body" into the vast, endless "realm" of "energy and thought forms" which underlies and somehow gives rise to the crude, "physical universe." The separation of the practitioner's astral body from its physical "housing" is not, however, total. A "connection" is "retained" by means of an "etheric cord" (Simos also calls it a "raith") through which the practitioner "feeds" while on his cosmic travels.

Other Wiccan accounts of the astral journey are essentially similar to Simos's. According to Warren-Clarke (1987, 41), the practitioner's ability to project his astral body "from one place to another" may be enhanced by a rigorous training of his imagistic powers. Farrar (1984, 214) informs us that we have "no cause to eat or drink" as we go, but "if we did drink ritual wine during astral projection it would be *astral* wine, manifested on the astral plane" by the traveler's "own willpower." Farrar remarks that astral projection is ultimately a kind of "bilocation," or the "gift of being able to be in two places at once." In helping us to see this, he offers a drawing of a naked woman lying on her back while another woman just like her, but of a slightly different color, arises out of her body and floats into the air.

What is particularly striking about astral projection is the degree to which it strives to actually reproduce and regain dualunity. One *was* "bilocated" at the inception of his life, existing in and through the mother as much as in and through himself. In a very special psychoanalytic sense, *one was two*. Here, one casts a magical circle around himself, goes into a trance, leaves the "physical housing" of his body, and psychically floats into a huge cosmic sea of primal energies to which he is connected by a "cord," an etheric, wraithlike unbilicus designed explicitly to "feed" him during the period of his projective altered state. And needless to say, one can do this over and over again, every day, for hours on end, should one wish to do so. The repressed, in this case the obsessional longing to re-fuse with the mother's body, has returned thinly disguised as a manifestation of one's "higher" or "spiritual" nature. Astral projection is, of course, practiced by occultists generally, not just by Witches, and it was indulged in long before the modern Witchcraft movement commenced (H. Carrington and S. Muldoon, 1929). It found its way to the Craft simply because it offered Witches a splendid opportunity to deny their separation from the caregiver. Ultimately, astral projection says to the Witch, "Do you want dual-unity? Do you want to exist again in the sphere of the all-encompassing mother? Well, lie down, close your eyes, and go for it!" When Simos (1979, 151) declares that we must return from our astral journey "slowly and gently," that "coming out" of our trancelike state is just as "important" as "going in," she merely touches upon the other side of the dual-unity equation. Having engaged in refusion with the object, or, in Mahler's terms, having "re-fueled" emotionally through our psychic umbilicus, we return to the "real world" secure in the knowledge that Mother-Goddess is there, dancing galactically in space and awaiting another visit from her charge when his affective hunger wells up within him again. Like all dual-unity games (going to church on Sunday, talking with God in prayer, etc.), astral travel is both toward and away from the object, a rhythmic regression and return to reality. The toward part of this game happens to be more fascinating and more challenging to us psychoanalytically because it stands at the edge of mental disturbance.

Visualization: Magic and Its Ends

Visualization, states Cunningham (1989, 82), "is the most basic and yet advanced technique called for in magic and Wicca," for it "programs the power" raised by the Witch "to create changes in this world" (84). More specifically, when the Witch feels himself "bursting with power," power that has been raised by "rubbing his palms together for twenty minutes, tensing his muscles, and breathing deeply," he "holds out his right (projective) hand, and directs his energy from his body, through his arm and out his fingers," all the while "using his visualization." "Really see and feel it streaming out," writes Cunningham, as you go about, say, sealing your house from evil. Simos (1979, 151) regards visualization as the means to discovering one's "place of power," a "new space" of being in which one feels "safe, protected, in complete control, and in touch with one's deepest sources of strength." In the words of Warren-Clarke (1987, 18), "those who choose the path of magic" will find visualization to be "the most important technique of all." This brings us to a pivotal assertion.

As we consider the psychoanalytic significance of these passages, we must not make the error of confusing the working of magic with its ends. I mean, it is tempting to regard the end—protecting a house from evil, recouping lost wealth, etc.—as the essential item in the activity, much as Malinowski does when he declares that all magic is a kind of emotional wishing for something, or Roheim (by implication at least) when he asserts that magic originates in infancy and is devoted to accomplishing unconscious purposes of an oral or oedipal nature. But the end, the wish, or the purpose is merely a kind of secondary bribe, and an ancillary consideration. What the doer of magic most deeply desires is to be in the position of doing magic, *to be in that state,* for it is *in* that state that he experiences refusion and the omnipotence of thought that accompanies refusion. It is *in* that state that he establishes, or better reestablishes, the lost and longed-for link with the object. In a very real sense, it makes no difference to the Wiccan magician what the aim of his magic is; anything will do, anything will interest him (barring, of course, obviously immoral requisitions), as long as he is able to *be magical,* as long as he is able to engage in activities that will give him the delicious, ecstatic feeling he knew formerly in the dual-unity situation when he was fused, omnipotent, and ever, ever so precious. That is why a Wiccan fortune-teller can appear to take an interest in the trivial affairs of ten thousand ridiculous clients; each time he goes to work he gets, in addition to his fee, the drug-like "hit" of feeling omnipotent and fused.

This applies to an enormous range of magical practices but is perhaps most vividly exemplified in scrying, or crystal gazing. As the Witch stares into her crystal ball she experiences *power,* power to master time and space, to know the secrets of the past and future both in the immediate location and far away. Moreover, the act of *staring* recalls unconsciously the primal, mutual face-gazing activity between mother and infant through which the latter's ego, with its rudimentary perceptions of space and time, was formed. Here is the dual-unity situation, with its fusion and omnipotence, all over again. Here is the mother-infant bond with its wondrous feelings of connection and power. No wonder Witches are traditionally hooked on staring into their crystal balls. To put the matter as bluntly as possible from the psychoanalytic perspective, the crystal ball of the Witch is the mother's face.

Polarity and Channeling

Magic is ultimately rooted, say Wiccans (Farrar 1984, 33), in the "polarity" of the universe. Positive-negative, female-male—when these interact we get power. On the higher, transcendent "levels," it is the union of "the Goddess and the God" (Farrar 1984, 33) that dramatically puts to work polarity's creative potential; on the "level" of human interaction polarity manifests itself in a thousand ways, from sexual congress to rubbing one's palms together in preparation for magic. Yet no matter what "level" is involved in producing power, the principle is the same. In Farrar's (1984, 33) words, which are echoed endlessly in the literature, "as above, so below." Thus, in the Wiccan view, all "levels" of existence, from spiritual to mundane, are ultimately connected as manifestations of a polarized cosmic design. What we do "down here" not only echoes but actually expresses what Goddess and God do "up there." And what Goddess and God do "up there" discovers its way to the human "level," and *is* the human "level" to the eye that can penetrate the core.

Certainly the production of energy in the world has something to do with what we choose to call positive and negative charges, or particles. We have all read simple descriptions of electrical devices, but to say these have something to do with the working of magic, or with the behavior of deities, or with the ultimate nature of the universe (if there is such a thing), is nothing more nor less than facile analogizing and fantasizing. Witches do not know the answer to such mysteries and so they make up "theories." Their projections, however, are not without interpretative value. Indeed, when we examine them from an analytic perspective, we find that they guide us quite nicely to the essentials of the matter. The "poles" from which magic arises are, quite simply, the before-separation and after-separation worlds, the "positive" feelings one has during the stage of omnipotence and fusion, and the "negative" feelings one has during the period of separation and differentiation, as described by Mahler. It is when *these* "levels" interact and when the urge to recapture the limitlessness of the early time meets the traumatic reality of one's separation and smallness, that the "energy" to do magic, or to *be magical again,* arises. The "power" of the Witch is a projective manifestation of the dynamic, conflicting objects of his inner world, the "positive" and "negative" forces that clash therein.

Nor is it a coincidence that Witches locate the cosmic power plant in the male and female "poles" of Goddess and God: When fusion subsides, when omnipotence ends, when separation and differentiation loom, it is the symbiotic world of the mother that the child must give up for the more socially oriented world of the paternal figure. *This* is the primal conflict. The Goddess and the God are simply the mother (the before-separation world) and the father (the after-separation world) "writ large," metaphoric or mythic expressions of the gods of the nursery. Witchcraft projects the paternal influence on a cosmic scale (as the small child is wont to do) and then turns to its own projection in a grandiose effort to explain its power-seeking, its thirst for omnipotence and fusion. In short, the Wiccan "theory" of polarity, rooted explicitly in the figures of Goddess and God, comprises a fairly obvious "Freudian slip." As for the Wiccan notion of "levels," and the traditional Wiccan causative formula, "as above so below," it merely discloses, through an additional slip, the manner in which the unconscious spins the plot here. What is happening "above," at the conscious level, in the projective metaphors and myths of the Craft, is indeed related integrally to what is occurring "below" the surface, at the "level" where old wishes and aims, tied to the parental figures or the gods of the nursery, will not be relinquished.

Note how the idea and practice of "channeling" perfectly illustrates the point. As the Priestess "draws down the moon," writes Farrar (1984, 67), she becomes the actual, physical "channel of the Goddess" who comes through her not in some diffuse, spiritual way but who really takes over a specific part of her body and manifests divine power through that. "Anybody who has witnessed Drawing Down the Moon regularly," states Farrar in another place (1987, 65), "must agree that it works. Time and time again, an 'ordinary' human woman seems transformed by it, so that the coven has no difficulty in reacting to her as the voice and the presence of the Goddess. . . . Nor is it just the matter of the tone of delivery. Many times we have known the familiar words of the Charge to be unexpectedly replaced by something quite different." And then, in words that beget our full analytic attention, "in either case, the delivery is not usually determined by the Priestess' conscious decision. Every experienced Priestess is familiar with the strange feeling of observing from a corner of her own mind, *of listening to the Goddess using her vocal cords, and wondering what will come next*" (Farrar 1987, 65; my emphasis). Clearly, the practice of "channeling" is designed to get the mother—in Wiccan terms the Goddess and in psychoanalytic terms the object—*back into the body of the practitioner, to have her dwelling therein once again.* During the early period, as we have seen, the infant and the caretaker are locked in a kind of "organ" relationship; the mother serves as a symbiotic organ of the baby, and the baby is attached to the mother as a neotenous, dependent facet of the *corpus maternus.* This is the dual-unity situation in which bodily boundaries do not yet exist, in which two human beings are physiological and emotional appendages of each other.

It is precisely when this unique situation ends, when dual-unity gives way to differentiation, when one becomes two and the child moves toward the cultural realm, that the "polarities" of human existence begin to emerge in earnest. Astral projection witnesses the Witch leaving the physical "house" of her body to join the Great Mother in the heavens; channeling, by contrast, draws the Goddess down into the "house" of the Witch where she proceeds to inhabit or take over a specific bodily part. In this way, both practices deny polarity (or pursue dual-unity) but from opposing psychological directions. As for the coven members in attendance while the "channeling" proceeds, they undergo the powerfully *transitional* experience of beholding the Priestess in the grip of the Great Mother, of witnessing a bodily organ of the Leader being usurped by a mythic version of the original caregiver. The Priestess' delusional conjuring up of the object into her own throat says to those who sit in awe around her: Dual-unity *can* be recaptured; polarity *can* be collapsed; we *can* feel the mother back in our bodies again; we *are* fused with the object in the most primitive, fundamental way— body with body, cell with very cell.

Even when an instance of channeling takes a form somewhat less intense than that which we witness in Farrar, even when the Goddess makes her presence felt in a more general way, the underlying psychodynamic configuration will be very much the same. The Witch will experience her being, her body, her "soul" as the expression has it, under the sway of the object and in the control of the object, and it is precisely that experience, that seductive, infantile experience, which the practice of channeling aims to induce.

Auras

Our bodies evidently give off some sort of electrical field that has been captured photographically by the Russian inventor Semyon Kirlian. We do not know exactly what this field consists of, let alone what it *means*. The entire matter is currently under investigation and the investigations (to put it mildly) are not leading us in any obvious direction (cf. Drury 1985, 143). All of this does not deter the Witches, however. They plunge right in with a variety of explanations and applications, and they do so because the so-called aura, like the so-called astral body, extends itself invitingly to the unconscious as a version of the dual-unity situation. A fine example emerges from a ritual that consecrates the athame, or sacred knife.

The athame "serves the Witch as a strength and defence in all magical operations against her enemies visible and invisible" (Farrar 1984, 44). It can be "conjured" by the names "Abrach and Abracadabra," and it can be consecrated through the "Great Gods and Gentle Goddesses." Having been conjured and suitably consecrated, the athame "should be handed to its new owner with a Fivefold Salute." In turn, the new owner should "press it against his body for a time to get the aura." The athame "should be in as close connection as possible to the naked body for at least a month, i.e., kept under the pillow, etc.," and must not come into contact with anyone else until it has been "thoroughly impregnated" with the owner's "aura." However, "a pair working together may own the same tools, which will be impregnated with the aura of both."

Farrar's "scientific" explanation for all this is straightforward enough. "Power is latent in the body and may be drawn out and used in various ways by the skilled" (Farrar 1984, 53). It "seems to exude from the body via the skin and possibly from the bodily orifices." Yet "unless it is confined in a circle it will be swiftly dissipated." Now, as we have been told over and over again by the Wiccan texts, the power of the body, like that of everything else in the universe, is ultimately an expression of the Goddess, indeed *is* the Goddess manifesting Herself energetically on the physical plan (Cunningham 1988, 20; Simos 1979, 138). Just as the Goddess can *touch us* and *change us* (Simos 1979, 175), so *we* can *touch* items to our bodies *in which the Goddess dwells* and experience a mighty change in those very items. The sword or athame gets power when pressed to the subject's skin because the subject still feels the omnipotent object residing beneath it.

The transformation or empowering of the athame, then, is an expression of the subject's belief in his own omnipotence, derived from the object of infancy extant in his inner world and assuming the projective form of "aura."

It is not only through an invisible transference of "power" that the aura expresses itself. On the contrary, it can be *seen,* and it is Simos (1979, 137), among others, who tells us how to see it. The "exercise," she writes, "is best practised in a group. Each of the members can take turns being the subject. All should be proficient at sensing the aura." Having set up a plain dark background, and having situated the naked subject against it, we dim the lights, relax, and in a "light state of trance . . . scan the space around the subject in search of a glowing line." To some, Simos continues, the aura will appear as a "cloudlike astral body"; to others it will appear simply "like a shadow, oddly lighter than the background"; and to others still it will manifest itself only as a "subtle difference between foreground and background." Yet all of us will see it as we "accustom ourselves to our astral vision" and "learn to see energy move." Simos concludes by reminding us that the "energy" of the aura is ultimately derived from the "great dance of the universe," which is to say, *from the Goddess.* Indeed, she closes her projections on this topic with the following words, addressed, of course, to the reader: "Thou art Goddess, eternally linked, connected, at one with the moving spirit of All" (138). What does this mean from a psychoanalytic angle?

Surrounding the Witch as a kind of psychic halo, the aura is, quite simply, a delusional version of the maternal object. Linked explicitly with the Great Goddess, it radiates the omnipotence and narcissistic admiration that the mother shined on the infant during the early period. Standing in front of her fellow coveners who, of course, validate the thing's existence through sheer group suggestibility (only those who are *predisposed* to finding auras should do this, Simos stated), the subject is given the chance to luxuriate again in the wondrous, inward glow she knew toward her life's inception, when the object resided at the center of her emotional and perceptual world. Equally significant, the aura's visibility, its "factual" presence, gives subject and coven members alike undeniable proof that separation and differentiation never really occurred. Not only is the Goddess present but She is attached to, *blended into* the subject (or vice versa). As Simos puts it, "thou art eternally linked to the All; thou art Goddess." Once more we see Witchcraft's obsessional effort to collapse ego boundaries, to unite the subject with a version of the caretaker, to restore dual-unity, to *deny separation*. When God became flesh in the person of Jesus, He afforded Christians the opportunity to see Him and know Him. Witchcraft goes one step further. Not only does it permit the adherent to see the Goddess in her divine form of radiating energy; it also permits him to fuse with Her, to *be* Her; Once again, "thou art Goddess." But there is still another purpose to which auras may be put.

Auric healing, states Farrar (1984, 228), is ultimately rooted in what the Hindus call Prâna, or "vitality." Although this "force" has not yet been recognized (let alone understood) by science, it is, Farrar assures us, "*the* vital force of the Cosmos." It "permeates our solar system (and certainly all others) and every living organism is charged with a concentration of it; without it we would not *be* living organisms. . . . The successful healer learns to draw on the surrounding free prâna and to recharge the patient with it." How does the "auric healer" go about this, exactly?

Employing his "clairvoyant power" to discover the "aura" of his patient, the healer "lays on his hands." It is "not the physical body on which the hands need to be laid," however; "the influence is from the aura of the healer's hands to the aura of the patient's body." Thus "experienced auric healers will not touch the patient's body during the laying on of hands; they will hold them an inch or two away, in contact with the aura." Let us say the patient has a headache. The healer will relax, begin to breathe "steadily and slowly," and then "envisage not only his lungs but every pore of his body drawing in prâna from the atmosphere." When he feels "sufficiently charged," he will hold his "healing hand" an inch or two from the patient's head and "*will* the accumulated prâna into [the patient's] aura to do its healing work and restore normality." Such is the essence of "auric healing."

What we notice first here is the correspondence between the Hindu "prâna" and the Wiccan "Goddess." As we have seen repeatedly in this chapter, the Craft regards the Goddess as "*the* vital force of the Cosmos," as "that which permeates the solar system and every living organism." When the auric healer "fills his pores" with the "prâna" of the world around him, he is psychically taking in (or "introjecting") yet another projective version of the caretaker, the internalized object of life's first years. To claim the universe, including its sentient creatures, is driven by some sort of energy or power, and then to call that energy or power "prâna" and regard it as an *explanation* of things, is exactly the same as saying that opium puts people to sleep because it contains a "dormative principle." Such "explanations" are mere verbal redundancies; they account for everything and for nothing at all. Hindus and Wiccans *feel* the truth of their "explanations," *know* the truth of them, because Hindus and Wiccans have already had the experience of existing in an environment where the invisible omnipotence of the maternal figure made everything *go*.

Having loaded his "aura" with "prâna," or, in analytic terms, having convinced himself thoroughly of his omnipotence, the auric healer allows the patient *to participate therein*. He tells him, in effect, I am omnipotent, magical, possessed of the Goddess' energy (prâna), and I am now going to share this incredible stuff with *you*. That the sharing transpires *aura to aura* rather than body to body (remember, the aura, too, is a projective version of the object) places the interaction squarely on the emotive-psychological, as opposed to the physical, plane. Aura to aura means simply unconscious to unconscious, or better, internalized object to internalized object. What all of this signifies to the patient is obvious enough: He finds himself once again in the dual-unity situation. An omnipotent presence is filling him with a compelling sensation of omnipotence. The *transference* is not "auric," but psychoanalytic; it is not "prâna" that the healer *wills* into the patient but the omnipotence of thought. Thus auric healing comprises a psychological *symbiosis* similar to the one that characterized the period of life during which the mother had only to hover over the infant to restore his equilibrium. Healer and patient cooperate in playing the dual-unity game together: one from the parental side of the equation, the other from the infantile side. Like astral projection and channeling, auric healing finds its way to Wicca because it permits adherents to rediscover the *magnetism* of the first relationship. It is not "normality" that is being "restored" here but the magical past. If the patient feels better after one of these sessions, it is because the terrible truths of separation and smallness have been temporarily taken away from him at the unconscious level, where his "headache" may well have originated. The very fact that the world still appears to contain omnipotent people may provide him with some comfort. As for the healer, he thirsted for omnipotence and fusion when the game began, when he decided to swell himself up with the Goddess' power (prâna). One would assume that by the game's conclusion (depending of course on the conduct of the patient), his thirst will have been gratified—for a while.

Does this imply there is no such thing as clairvoyance? Of course not, anymore than it implies there is no such thing as willpower. The world contains a good many intuitive, gifted individuals who are able to perceive, or "see into," other people and events in ways that are truly remarkable, even mysterious. But we are not dealing with that here. We are dealing, rather, with individuals who go about the world possessed of an exaggerated, narcissistic belief in their own omnipotence, their limitless capacity to affect the cosmos, to acquire power. We are dealing with the regressive, transitional need to reestablish the old dual-unity situation, to reparticipate in the *corpus maternus*, to deny separation and what we can call ordinary, everyday smallness and aloneness.

Farrar (1984, 203) helps us enormously when she declares that clairvoyance or mystical insight does not derive merely from the "unconscious," from that portion of a person's "psyche" which is "beyond the reach of waking awareness," but from "the life of another being" who resides "within" the clairvoyant, "still there, still active, still thinking." This "inner being," states Farrar, is properly regarded as the "guardian angel," a "mighty invisible companion" who continually tells us to *"listen, listen!"* It is "this commandment," Farrar concludes, that constitutes "the secret of clairvoyance."

Here again is that peculiar combination of *dependence* and *grandiosity* which characterizes the Craft as a whole. The "inner being" to whom Farrar refers, the "guardian angel" to whom we should "listen," is, on the one hand, a kind of imaginary companion or inward transitional presence modeled projectively upon the "angel" of the early period, the internalized caretaker who is "still there, still active, still thinking" our thoughts for us as we go about the world ostensibly "on our own." To put it another way and to get at this side of the matter as directly as we can, there is a striking unconscious similarity between the "guardian angel" and the nurturing, protective aspect of the Goddess upon whom the Witch emotionally depends and with whom she wants continually and obsessively to fuse. On the other hand, the conviction that one goes about the world accompanied on the inside by a "mighty invisible companion" who affords one uncanny, mystical insights into other people and events comprises yet another instance of the Witch's inclination to indulge in the omnipotence of thought, to consider herself special, wondrous, magical, limitless—a consideration that obviously compensates (or tries to compensate) for the huge dependency at work in her worship of the Goddess, in her constant, pressing need to reenter the *corpus maternus*. What Farrar calls Witchcraft's "secret of clairvoyance" is nothing more nor less than this: the hopeful, willful belief that one still enjoys the glow of the object's protection, and still retains a share of the object's power.

Numbers

Modern Witchcraft is awash in numbers. It ascribes them to the heavenly bodies, and to all manner of magical and/or ritualistic behaviors in an effort to increase their effectiveness. During the course of a healing ritual, for example, one might invoke the Goddess three times instead of once in keeping with the notion that the number for healing is three. Simos (1979, 207) tells us that the "number" for "Mars" is "2, 3, 16, or possibly 5." Accordingly, if Mars appears to be influencing one's chances for success during the performance of a particular rite, one might consider repeating specific aspects of that rite "2, 3, 16, or possibly 5" times, thus exerting a measure of control upon the planet.

The Wiccan "mood" in regard to numbers is captured by a passage from Gardner's *Book of Shadows* cited in Farrar (1984, 52):

> It is not meet to make offering of less than two score lashes to the Goddess, for here be a mystery. The fortunate numbers be 3, 7, 9 and thrice 7 which be 21. And these numbers total two score, so a less perfect or fortunate number would not be a perfect prayer. Also the Fivefold Salute be 5, yet it be 8 kisses; for there be 2 feet, 2 knees, and 2 breasts. And 5 times 8 be two score. Also there be 8 Working Tools and the Pentacle be 5; and five eights are two score.

The phony, "archaic" English of this passage is, by the way, entirely Gardner's invention. Although Warren-Clarke (1987, 47–50) does not have the space to give us "a full layout of numerology," she does manage to show us how through numbers we may discover the "key" to our "destiny," as well as a way to bring about personal "change." For the most part, it is a matter of writing our names down, assigning specific numbers to the letters, figuring in our date of birth, and then adding and subtracting in the light of a "Numerology Chart" that guides us toward the spiritual realm. "Because all things are vibrational," writes this author, "they can be reduced to numbers," numbers that "have connections with all other aspects of the occult."

Discussing patients who suffer a "disturbance of the time sense," Arlow (1984, 15) notes that the "dissynchronous patterns of the child's needs and the mother's availability inevitably introduce the factor of frustration." Time becomes a "representative of realistic necessity" and of the "frustrations experienced at all levels of subsequent sexual development." Thus the "roots of rebellion" against the "tyranny of the clock" extend far back into the individual's past. Indeed, notes Arlow (16), our "notions of time follow inexorably from early experiences with word concepts." The child "hears that time flies, flows, marches, crawls, and stands still. Time brings and time takes away." Now, "during the same period, the child also learns to count." Numbers, like time, "bind the child to reality and help to further the process of socialization. The child soon learns that each moment of time is assigned a specific and unalterable number in the history of eternity." However—and we come here to the crucial insight— "while time and causality are irreversible, numbers are not. Numbers can be moved in either direction. They can be extended, contracted, fractioned, and reversed. The fact that numbers can be manipulated at will endows them with a special appeal in the endless quest for omnipotence." It is "not surprising to see," Arlow concludes, "how prominent a role numerology plays in systems of magic." These remarks guide us nicely toward the psychoanalytic essence of Wicca's interest in numbers.

The "key" to the Witch's "destiny" is precisely the same as the "key" to everyone else's, namely what happened to her during the course of her development when symbiosis, with its attendant omnipotence and fusion, gave way to separation, differentiation, the rapprochement struggle, and the subsequent oedipal and adolescent periods. What we can call the Wiccan numbers game is an attempt to set all this aside, to claim that the tie to the omnipotent object is still intact, still functioning, still endowing the Witch with the power to determine not only the course of future events but the very meaning of planetary motion. As Arlow makes plain, numbers take the Witch back to the time when symbiosis was disrupted and lost. To the extent that the numbers game ties the Witch to the internalized object, it comprises, like the channeling game, or the astral travel game, or the auric healing game, but another version of the dual-unity game played out obsessively in an effort to restore an idealized, longed-for version of the past. As far as "destiny" is concerned, if one chooses to persist in the numbers game, or in any of the dual-unity games that characterize modern Witchcraft, one's destiny will be quite simply to remain fixed in regressive behaviors that give expression to unresolved infantile conflicts—in a word, to never grow up. Of course the Witch may regard the numbers game as something new and remarkable in her life, but there is really nothing new or remarkable about it. The concerns it addresses and the manner in which it strives to handle events and issues are an old story, reaching back into the initial stages of the Witch's existence. What appears new is old, what seems fresh and exciting is ultimately stale and neurotically obsessive. How did F. Scott Fitzgerald express it on the final page of *The Great Gatsby*? "So we beat on, boats against the current, borne back ceaselessly into the past."

Some Wiccan (and Human) Paradoxes

Everywhere in the literature of the Craft one comes upon statements that indicate a passionate concern with ecological, political, and feminist issues. "Witchcraft can be seen as a religion of ecology," declares Simos (1979, 10). Its goal is "harmony with nature, so that life may not just survive, but thrive." We must "save" the earth from destruction, writes Farrar (1987, 111); we must "watch over it, protect its fruits, and guard against those who would lay it waste." Witches hate "commissars and fascists," asserts Gerald Gardner (1959, 130); "there is no room for this sort of spirit in the Witch cult." According to Simos (1979, 7), Witchcraft stands on the side of American democracy; it is devoted to protecting freedom of speech, and to promoting both decentralized government and individual rights. Witchcraft opposes "discrimination" in any shape or form, especially discrimination against women, states Warren-Clarke (1987, 134). One of its chief purposes is to forge a society in which women may "liberate themselves" from old, patriarchal prejudices and enjoy full equality and wholeness as human beings (Simos 1979, 57). Indeed, Witchcraft urges women to forge their own identities aggressively, to gain their fair share of power and respect, and to heal the wounds inflicted upon them by men over the centuries (Simos 1979, 189). The question is, how does all this jibe with the regressive, magical thinking, the longing for fusion and omnipotence, the narcissistic grandiosity and outright mumbo jumbo, in short the *infantilism* that we have been exploring in this chapter.

Like cults, religions, and cultural institutions generally, Witchcraft appeals to all the levels of an individual's psychosexual development. It is both *toward* and *away from* the object of the early period. As we know, the Craft's magical systems speak powerfully to preoedipal and oedipal wishes, to the longing for fusion and omnipotence, to the hunger for a harmonious, reconstituted family. In its cultic status and fringe, rebellious nature, Wicca manages to address significant adolescent concerns. It "stands aside from the mainstream of society," writes Simos (1979, 19), scorning the "fruits of monetary success," and identifying with "artists, poets, shamans, mystics, and visionaries." At what we can call the adult level of realistic biological and social responsibility, Witches express genuine, ego-syntonic concern with environmental and political issues, with the need for careful stewarding of the planet and with the widespread, growing call for the just and decent treatment of all human beings, regardless of race or gender. Thus a second question arises: If Witches are able at one level of their psychosexual development to work constructively for the good of the world, why should we bother about their regressive, obsessive, infantile behaviors? Why not leave the Witches alone?

First and most obviously, there is the normal intellectual responsibility one feels to point out superstition, irrationality, and hokum when he believes he has come upon them. To discharge this responsibility is to afford devotees of the Goddess a chance to view their conduct from a fresh perspective, but that is only a happy spin-off of the central purpose. The writer can no more ignore what he considers to be regressive, infantile behavior on the part of a group claiming religious and philosophical legitimacy and working to establish a foothold in the cultural scheme of things than he can pretend not to notice a full eclipse of the sun while out walking on a bright summer day. Second, to live in the shadow of the object, to pursue omnipotence, grandiosity, and fusion, to go about the planet in the belief that one is magical, limitless, wondrous, special, is to increase the potential for disorder in the world. It is to keep all the old, irrational, mad forces alive and available to those who know how to use them for their own grandiose, egotistical ends. This is not to suggest that the ancient, patriarchal, Judeo-Christian setup is preferable to Wicca. It is not. But that does not make Wicca a desirable alternative. Indeed, *both* of these schemes come from different aspects of the *same* psychological place. The Judeo-Christian setup is tied neurotically to the father. The Wiccan alternative (matriarchy, etc.) is tied neurotically to the mother. What the world needs is *detachment* from the objects of the inner realm, detachment from those inward energies that seek to actualize the impossible, infantile aims of the early period, detachment from the unconscious agenda that is born aggressively and passionately in the crises of separation and differentiation through which all of us are fated to go. If we are capable of improvement as human beings, it will come as we see, clearly see, the degree to which our present "magical" goals are unconsciously connected to developmental events that transpired toward the inception of our lives, and accordingly *give them up.* For it makes no sense, to this writer at least, to work *realistically* for social and political progress on the one hand and to *deny reality* on a broad, massive scale on the other.

Much the same thinking may be brought to bear on the morality of Witchcraft, for here, too, we see the mix of reason and unreason, maturity and infantilism, acceptance and denial of reality that characterizes Wicca as a whole. For example, the most popular moral maxim of the Craft, often expressed in a defiant fashion, states that one is free to do whatever he wishes as long as he does not harm anyone else. Farrar (1984, 135) puts the matter this way, echoing the bogus, antique style of Gardner's *Book of Shadows:* "Eight words the Wiccan Rede fulfil, / And it harm none, do what you will."

Imagine the reaction of Socrates, Aristotle, or Kant to this sort of simpleminded nonsense. For how can a morality be based upon a position that ignores the responsibility of the individual to himself? If one "harms" oneself, might it not have a deleterious effect upon others? Are all people islands? Is not the individual a part of the community, and is not the community diminished when the individual behaves self-inimically? What exactly constitutes "harm" to another? And is the amount of "harm" *always* sufficient to curtail an individual's wish? Are not some things very harmful, and other things not so harmful? Where does one draw the line? If I am doing something important to me, and another person for neurotic reasons claims I am harming him, do I automatically desist? Who *judges* "harm"? Do not individuals, groups, and societies need judges? How do we address this problem in terms of the "Wiccan Rede"?

I won't continue. Not only does the literature of the Craft ignore such issues, but the reader has by this time, I suspect, recognized the inadequacy of a moral position that looks to others, as opposed to the self, for what we may term the moral foundation.

By contrast, the insistence of the Wiccan community that theirs is a morality based not upon the punitive, paternal superego but upon the nurturing and love associated with the figure of the Great Mother raises crucial considerations. "The model of the Goddess fosters respect for all living things," writes Simos (1979, 10); "it is not a parallel structure to the symbolism of God the Father." Hence "Wiccan ethics are positive rather than prohibitive. The morality of Witchcraft is far more concerned with 'blessed is he who' than with 'thou shalt not.' The extremes of masochistic asceticism and gross materialism seem to the Witch to be two sides of the same coin, because both distort human wholeness. . . . All living creatures are our siblings, different but related offspring of the same womb" (Farrar 1984, 135). Such an emphasis calls to mind the wholesale rethinking of moral issues that is currently taking place in the psychoanalytic community.

Questioning the accuracy and the value of Freud's moral theory, Eli Sagan (1988, 9) observes that the "dependence of the superego on the *particular* society in which it exists underlines a fatal flaw in the theory of the superego as representing the *moral* function within the psyche." Far from carrying out the task of morality in the mind, Sagan continues, "the superego is essentially *amoral* and can be as easily immoral as moral. Within a slave society, the superego legitimates slavery. Within a racist or sexist society, the superego demands racism and sexism. And in a Nazi society, the superego commands one to live up to genocidal ideals." Throughout the course of history a corrupt superego has been the norm, not the exception. Indeed, "most of the worst troubles that humankind has brought upon itself, including warfare, are impossible without the functioning of the superego" which we must finally regard as a kind of psychological "disease" (13). Unlike the superego, however, the "conscience knows clearly which actions are moral and which immoral"; the conscience is "incapable of corruption and pathology. It may be silenced or paralyzed, but one can never accurately speak of a diseased conscience." Furthermore—and we come here to the key consideration—the conscience "does not have to wait until the child's fourth or fifth year to make its presence felt. *Conscience has its origins in the basic nurturing situation,* and identification with the nurturer plays an essential role in its composition. Traditionally it is the mother, not the father, who presides over the birth of conscience, over the beginnings of morality" (p. 14; my emphasis). Because Freud was unwilling to look closely at the child's first relationship with the mother, he failed to extend his discussion of Eros to the place of its origin. Putting the matter in a nutshell, Sagan (176) writes, "identification with the nurturer is essential for psychic health because it is the only effective defense against the destructive drives." To protect the world's environment, to foster respect for all living creatures "great and small," we must strive for what the Witches would call a Goddess-centered morality and for what Sagan would call a morality grounded in the preoedipal, mother-child situation.

The point of the last distinction is that we do not *need* "the Goddess" and all the regressive, magical thinking that surrounds "the Goddess" to find our moral way. Just as we can shed this kind of baggage in the ecological and political spheres so we can shed it in the moral sphere too. We can spy the origins of morality in the actual circumstances and events of our own lives with our own mothers, as opposed to the supernatural realm with its mythic entities. We can have Witchcraft's wholesome moral emphasis without the narcissism, grandiosity, and omnipotence of thought that accompany the wish to reenter the *corpus maternus* and that feed the world's troublesome appetite for irrational behavior. In my view, our actual lives, our actual bodies, our actual experiences serve as a stronger, firmer foundation for morality than the projective expressions of the psyche. Moreover, to foster detachment from the objects of the inner world does not mean that we lose our capacity to love and nurture others. It means simply that we strive to *see* the origins and the significance of our emotional goals. It means that we stop identifying automatically with the passionate, narcissistic urges that well up within us, particularly when we are told by other people that we are Goddess-like and wonderful. Again in my view, our capacity for compassion and care can only be *enhanced* as we develop the courage to work through the crises of separation and loss in which our longing for fusion and omnipotence was born. Earlier we established Witchcraft's tendency to *deny* separation and loss. Perhaps we begin to perceive fully now the negative consequences of such a denial. Genuine confrontation with the self is the only true basis of morality.

Gender

"Through the Goddess," declares Simos (1979, 7), women can "reclaim their right, as women, to be powerful, to explore their own strengths and realizations." They can "enlighten their minds, celebrate their emotions, and more beyond their narrow, constricting roles." Indeed, "through the Goddess," women can become "inspired to see their aggression as healthy, and their anger as purifying." The Goddess is also "important for men," Simos (9) continues; "the oppression of men in Father God-ruled patriarchy is perhaps less obvious but no less tragic than that of women." Men are encouraged "to identify with a model no human being can successfully emulate: to be minirulers of narrow universes"; they are "at war with themselves" and "internally split"; they "lose touch with their feelings and their bodies, and become successful male zombies." It is "the Goddess," concludes Simos (10), who "allows men to experience the feminine side of their nature, which is often felt to be the deepest and most sensitive aspect of the self." The texts of the Craft abound with similar passages (cf. Warren-Clarke 1987, 66; Farrar 1984, 161; Cabot 1989, 15).

Carol Gilligan (1982, 6) observes in a crucial discussion of gender differences that the tendency of psychological theorists "to project a masculine image" onto human development "goes back at least to Freud, who built his theories ... around the experiences of the male child that culminate in the Oedipus complex." This tendency has of late been rectified in psychoanalysis by a variety of writers including Nancy Chodorow (1978), Robert Stoller (1964), and, of course, Gilligan herself. It boils down to the following: By the time a child is three, "the unchanging core of personality formation is with rare exception firmly and irreversibly established for both sexes" (Gilligan 1982, 7). Given that for both sexes "the primary caretaker in the first three years is typically female, the interpersonal dynamics of gender formation are different for boys and girls." Female identity formation "takes place in a context of ongoing relationship since mothers tend to experience their daughters as more like, and continuous with, themselves." Thus girls, in identifying themselves as female, "experience themselves as like their mothers, fusing the experience of attachment with the process of identity formation." By contrast, "mothers experience their sons as a male opposite," and boys, "in defining themselves as masculine, separate their mothers from themselves," thereby "curtailing their primary love and sense of empathic tie." Male development "entails a more emphatic individuation and a more defensive firming of ego boundaries." Girls emerge "with a stronger basis for experiencing another's needs or feelings as one's own. . . . Furthermore, girls do not define themselves in terms of the denial of preoedipal relational models [fusion] to the same extent as do boys. Therefore, regression to these modes tends not to feel as much a basic threat to their ego." In this way, "male gender identity is threatened by intimacy while female gender identity is threatened by separation. . . . Males tend to have difficulty with relationships, while females tend to have problems with individuation, competitive achievement, and success." In a passage that summarizes the central thrust of her theoretical position, Gilligan (17) writes, "women not only define themselves in a context of human relationship but also judge themselves in terms of their ability to care. Women's place in man's life cycle has been that of nurturer, caretaker, and helpmate, the weaver of those networks of relationships on which she in turn relies. But while women have thus taken care of men, men have, in their theories of psychological development, as in their economic arrangements, tended to assume or devalue that care." These stereotypes "reflect a conception of adulthood that is itself out of balance, favoring the separateness of the individual self over connection to others" and an "autonomous life of work" over "the interdependence of love and care." The bulk of Gilligan's subsequent discussion is devoted to exploring this "imbalance" in particular men and women.

It is precisely the rectification of this imbalance, in both females and males, that Witchcraft seems bent upon accomplishing. As we have just seen, Wiccan texts tell women not to fear competition and aggression, and not to believe that their capacity to care conflicts with the expression of so-called masculine traits. Men are told to develop their empathetic, caring, sensitive natures and not to succumb to the cultural stereotype of what constitutes a "real man." Can anyone fail at this juncture to see the ironic contradiction in all this? At the same time that Witchcraft asks women to be strong and independent it also asks them to reenter the *corpus maternus,* to merge dependently with an obvious, full-blown, projective image of the mother— the Great Goddess. At the same time that Witchcraft asks women to rely on themselves, to discover their genuine inner resources, it also asks them to rely on magic and magical invocations, to consider themselves gifted and precious because they have relinked psychologically with the *magna mater.* Surely it counts for something psychoanalytically that the texts of the Craft typically include invocations such as the following: "Come Mama! come into our circle, our womb, be with us now, Mama, be with us now!" (Simos 1979, 89). Thus the Craft takes women in two opposing emotional directions. No matter how cleverly its advocates rationalize and explain this antithesis, it must ultimately have a confusing, stultifying effect on the female psyche.

As for men, Witchcraft asks them to indulge their caring, sensitive, feminine side and to relax their fears of boundary violation at the same time that it plays upon those very fears by urging them to re-fuse with the Great Mother, to reestablish the preoedipal symbiosis they strove so mightily, as males, to relinquish. "Mother of all life, engulf us with your love, sweep us away!" cries another Wiccan invocation (Simos 1979, 73, 105). Surely this goes beyond a mere increase of one's empathetic capabilities. What the Craft is encouraging in men here is precisely what it is encouraging in women, namely regression to an earlier stage of psychosexual development in which the symbiotic bond to the caretaker remains intact. I cannot see what good such a denial of separation and differentiation will do anyone, be he male, female, or a combination of both. But even more contradictory and ironic is the following: At the same time that Wicca asks men to rein in their lust for power, their urge to control others and to enhance their material wealth, it offers them a variety of magical techniques for increasing their power, for increasing their control over people and objects, indeed for actualizing their omnipotence. Again and again it reminds them, following Aleister Crowley, that "magic is the Science and Art of causing change to occur in conformity with Will" (cf. Adler 1986, 8), and that Wicca is the way to discover precisely that science and art. It is not only women that Witchcraft is fated to confuse. Men must come in for their share of emotional befuddlement too.

A final word on the Wiccan texts: Of the many compelling psychological realizations they offer us, the most outstanding perhaps is that the only real magic is the magic of honest self exploration, the magic of no magic at all.

Part Two: Three Witches and a Coven Meeting

What follows is meant to be read only in the light of the context. I cannot control the reader, but I will say emphatically that unless he has digested the discussion to this point he will miss a great deal. I present my interviews and experiences directly and offer no analytic comments or interpretations. I want the material to speak for itself. As we have seen, an individual's involvement in the Craft may engage all the levels of his psychosexual development. It can be heavily imbued with the wishes of infancy, with the longing for omnipotence and merger; it can display a rebelliousness and a search for identity, characteristics we commonly associate with adolescence; and it can evince a mature, genuine concern with social and environmental issues, that is, the quest for justice, equality, and a pollution-free planet. Typically, all of these levels are operative in the Witch, but *some are considerably more operative than others in individual cases,* as I believe my materials will show. The coven meeting, too, will challenge the reader's ability to explore what I may presume to call "the data" in a fluid, multileveled way. Finally, I have worked in all cases to conceal the subjects' identities without altering the substance of my notes and tapes. While I have perforce done some editing, I have also attempted to leave things pretty much as they were presented to me, even at the risk of some repetition and disorganization. For psychoanalysis, of course, disorganization and repetition sometimes disclose unconscious intention, and I did not want to sacrifice that potential to a flawless narrative flow.

Natalie

I met Natalie around 1:00 in the afternoon at a small Spanish restaurant in Richmond, a municipality of greater Vancouver. She was a tall, slender woman of thirty-two, with dark hair and eyes, a glowing, olive complexion, and graceful, athletic movements. Attired in a gray running suit and a pair of white sneakers, she spoke of her quest for a master's degree in counseling psychology and of her interest in therapeutic massage. After chatting amicably for a few moments, we commenced the interview.

MDF: Tell me a little bit about your background, your family, religious beliefs, and so on.

Natalie: I was born in Winnipeg. My family was heavily into Christianity (United Church of Canada), and I was obliged to attend services from an early age. I never really took to it. I mean, I was never drawn into the religious ideas and feelings of the church. It just wasn't me. I was confirmed at fourteen but I can remember that by the time I was fifteen

I found the whole thing ridiculous, and quit. I guess I resented having to attend Sunday school and services all
those years, so it felt really good to chuck it.

MDF: Were your parents upset?

Natalie: Yes. I can remember the quarrels we had about my not
going to church anymore, but I should clarify that my dad
died when I was eight and that by the time of my confirma-
tion I was living with my mom and my stepdad who also
claimed to be a believer.

MDF: How did you get on with your stepdad?

Natalie: Not very well. I think I resented his intrusion and I felt he
was rather wishy-washy compared to dad who was more
decisive, more involved in the family, although mom was
always the real center of things. I can remember trying to
get much closer to mom and to my brother after dad died
and I guess I saw my stepdad as interfering with that.

MDF: What do you mean, mom was really the center?

Natalie: She was just always at the hub of things, like the central
post office where you have to go to pick up the really important stuff. I was always close to her and always relied
on her. A few years ago when I went into therapy I realized
I may have been too close to mom, sort of enmeshed in
her. She told me how to live, how to be; and yet at the same
time I always had the feeling I was the center *for her,* like
she lived through *me* and *my brother* during the time I
thought I was living through *her.* When I had therapy, mom
used to come to some of my sessions because my therapist
said we had a lot of separation work to do. It came out that
mom was a rather anxious person, not very happy in her
marriage, and not very happy in her sex life.

MDF: Do you see your mom very often now?

Natalie: She's dead. She died four years ago.

MDF: What about your stepdad and brother?

Natalie: My brother is in therapy, and we're having our problems,
but I seem to be getting on better with my stepdad, although I don't see him much. We went to dinner together
a few weeks ago and we both got a little drunk on wine. He
asked me, with his hand on my arm, if we ever did anything
naughty together when I was young. I said I didn't think
so. Then he told me I was very beautiful and that he would
"f——" me at the drop of a hat. We were both drunk by
then, but that wasn't unusual. There was a fair bit of drinking, mostly secretive, in my family, in spite of the Christian
beliefs. Mom, too. For the past year, in fact, I have been
going to AA meetings in an effort to get past this thing.

When I say AA I mean AA for gays and lesbians. I'm now a lesbian.

MDF: Would you be willing to tell me about that?

Natalie: I had lots of boyfriends as a teenager but nothing seemed to go well. In my early twenties I lived with different men but again it wasn't very successful. I was always unhappy and somehow dissatisfied. Then I met Karen. She was teaching at a college I attended, and we began to spend a lot of time together, eventually including weekends. We have an equal, open relationship; it has its ups and downs, but we've been together for nearly three years now and I have the feeling it will go on for a while.

MDF: Tell me something about your involvement in Witchcraft. How did it begin?

Natalie: I confess my involvement in organized Witchcraft has been waning of late. It's a long story, but my interest has always been in new age thinking, women's issues, the environment, politics. Witchcraft sort of entered into these more than I entered into Witchcraft. I've been a feminist for several years. But I've always had spiritual or even mystical inclinations, too. My family background has some Celtic in it so naturally I have always been interested in healing, something Witches do. Anyway, a few years ago I went to the Witches' camp in the Gulf Islands [near Vancouver] during August. Starhawk [Miriam Simos] was there and many other accomplished Wiccans. The camp was great. After a while I felt completely at home with these people. They seemed able to harmonize everything; I mean spiritual, political, feminist, ecological. It all came together, including *play,* in one total expression of feeling. By the end of two weeks I'd decided to become a Witch. I don't mean that I wanted to gaze into crystal balls or say abracadabra with a pointed hat on. For me, the main things are feminism, the environment, and peace. But I felt connection there; I felt I belonged. These were my kind of people, and I wanted to be with them. I returned to Vancouver, was initiated, and joined a coven. As time went on, however, some problems developed.

MDF: How is that?

Natalie: I have a strong need for conflict resolution, and I find that the coven and the Witches can be superficial in that respect. They deny things and project things. They use the Craft and the group to act-out their own shit. I began to get ambivalent about the coven almost from the very beginning. Maybe that was because I am a strong feminist and environmentalist, with a political orientation. I mean, I never had any big conversion experience as such, even when I was initiated. That doesn't mean I don't have a strong spiritual nature, though. I've had mystical moments all my life and feel as capable as any Witch in this respect. When mom died I underwent several very powerful altered states, real mystical experiences in which I felt joined to her; and I got this, too, after breakups with men, the feeling we were still together, although eventually I was able to let go of them. I can still find mom when I really need her. I meditate, to relax and center, and also to find those I need, mom mainly. I also feel very connected to the earth. I've always felt this way. It's a warm, glowing feeling all through me, like I really have a connection.

MDF: Could you amplify this?

Natalie: For me, the earth is a living body, a living entity, an organism; Witches call it Goddess, and I regard myself as an eco-feminist here. I believe that the earth is alive, that it is the mother of all life, that it must be saved from the polluters, and that men should see the female as central, and stop treating women badly, just using them. I actually hug trees, hug them as part of the earth's body, and I get warm feelings with my arms around them. When mom died, I went to the beach and felt this tie to nature. I knew I wasn't alone. I was linked to the world—more than to people, who aren't like nature to me. I often don't feel I'm really part of the community. People just do too much denying and projecting. They dump on you and try to control you. I feel more a part of nature, more at home in nature than with other people. I left the coven because of the games and the denial. People are all clammed-up. They don't say what they mean; they don't even *know* what they mean. The coven was a lot of aggressive games and conflict, when what I wanted was mediation.

MDF: What were the circumstances surrounding your departure from the coven?

Natalie: Gloria, the High Priestess, wanted everyone's power. That's really all she was after. At first I deferred to her and shut up. I let her know through my expressions and bodily posture that she could have power from me. I suppressed myself and gave her the power. That's all power is, actually. It is regard, the projection of energy into another person through regard. She loved it, from everyone. She was like an actress, all dressed up in exotic clothes and jewelry, playing the part of Priestess in a theatrical way, more like a movie star than the leader of a religious group. And she wanted hierarchy. She wanted a court, with favorites and servants. Eventually I couldn't stand it and so I began to take my power back. My expressions and body language said I was taking it back and she noticed right away. A few weeks later there was an explosion. I told her she was a phony, an insincere manipulator. She hated me, although she pretended not to, like I was a poor crazy person. I had to leave the group, of course, and I don't want to rejoin it or any other group right now. When I see her, she smiles and pretends to be friendly but it's all BS. I don't trust her, or the other coven members. They saw it all, and they see her for what she is, too, but they don't say anything. They just go on with the show, the projective games, the master-slave thing. They're silent. They won't take sides.

MDF: But you still practice, do you not?

Natalie: Yes; I practice on my own. Gloria wrote me a twenty-page letter accusing me of disloyalty and all sorts of things; it was another psychological game, but very aggressive. I didn't answer. I'm going more and more into psychology now, getting away from the projection and the denial— what I call the BS. And I also feel more and more drawn to the nature groups, the Greens, Greenpeace, Friends of the Earth, organizations like that. As I see it, the spiritual, psychological, and environmental all go together, as part of the same effort to improve our situation on the earth. I'm planning a trip into the bush, a retreat; that seems more meaningful to me now than a coven meeting.

MDF: Tell me more about your solitary practice as a Witch. What do you do, typically, and how often?

Natalie: It varies, but I usually practice about once a week, in my living room. I begin by making a circle, tracing it on the floor with a stick or knife. Sometimes as I trace the circle I hum or sing. Then I do the directions. I ask the spirit of the North to be here, then the spirit of the West and South and East. I ask them to bring me healing energy, to take away my tension. When that's done I take water with salt in it (I think of it as spiritual sea water) and rub it on my face and body to cleanse and purify. After relaxing for a few moments, or perhaps grounding (which means feeling my connection to the earth), I invoke the Goddess from the center of my circle. I ask Her to come into my sacred space, to be with me in my circle.

MDF: How do you know when She comes?

Natalie: I feel a shift in energy. I feel powerful, centered, peaceful, grounded. I feel complete in the circle with the Goddess, like there's a ribbon around me, a place for me to be and feel good in.

MDF: Anything else?

Natalie: I feel I get the power to take risks when I am in the circle. I feel I can do things I would not ordinarily be able to do, at work or in university. I mean, assert myself in situations with other people, which I now do. The good feelings in the circle also lead me to meditate. I sit quietly for a few minutes and think about the things I want to accomplish. I sometimes chant, or sing, or image the people and situations that please me. This is usually the last thing I do, or almost the last thing.

MDF: What do you mean?

Natalie: I always thank the Goddess for coming to me. I know she leaves at the end, but I *hope* she stays. I ask her to stay with me even though the rituals are over. And I thank the directions for their gifts, just as I thank the Goddess. All that remains, of course, is to banish the circle, but for me, saying goodbye to the directions *is* banishing the circle. This doesn't mean I feel suddenly disconnected, however. The feeling of connection can go on for hours. I once felt the Goddess' presence for an entire weekend.

MDF: I understand that Wiccan gatherings can be very colorful and very moving. Don't you ever want to practice with others? Is this all you need?

Natalie: Occasionally I mull over the idea of going to a festival, or sabbat, or group meeting, but I haven't been doing that. Right now it feels good to be on my own. I feel more like working with a few women on the environment, or on some political issues. My therapy seems to be heading me in that direction. I'll just have to see what happens down the road.

Richard

I met Richard at his rented home in Kitsilano, a quiet neighborhood of tree-lined streets and older framed houses in the Victorian style about two miles south of downtown Vancouver. It was 1:30 in the afternoon, and Richard, casually dressed in jeans and a black t-shirt, was babysitting his twin daughters who were in the midst of their afternoon nap. Thirty-eight years old, of medium height and build, with brown eyes behind gold wire glasses, and rather long, straight brown hair, Richard was currently spending his days writing a Wiccan newsletter and attempting to organize a coven of which he was to be the leader. His common-law wife was working as a registered nurse, and, according to Richard, resisting his attempts to involve her in the Craft. This seemed to annoy him. After chatting over herbal tea for fifteen minutes or so, we began the interview.

MDF: Tell me a little bit about your background, your family, religious persuasion—that sort of thing.

Richard: I was born in Hamilton [Ontario] in 1952. My mother belonged to the Anglican Church and was fairly devout. She attended services regularly, involved herself in church activities, and enrolled me in Sunday school which I attended for several years, until I was twelve. My father was of no particular religious persuasion. He stayed clear of all that, but I believe he and my mother were involved in a serious conflict over the role of religion in the family. And over other things as well. They had a very stormy marriage, with lots of quarreling and weekly threats of separation or divorce. Much of this obviously stemmed from my father's drinking. He was a full-fledged alcoholic, constantly drunk, constantly storming around like an animal, scaring the hell out of us day in and day out. When I was eleven he left, for good.

MDF: How did you feel about this?

Richard: Do you mean was I upset? Not at all! I wanted him to leave. He was a self-blinded man, closed off, defensive, violent, and unable to give or receive affection. I haven't seen or heard from him since, and I have no desire for contact. I'm not saying it was easier after he left, only that it was less scary. I don't know how my mom managed to raise us all during those years. I was the eldest of six children, two brothers and three sisters, and it seemed we got by mostly on part-time jobs, severe restraint, and some governmental assistance. I'm very grateful to my mother for hanging in there. I tried to help out as much as I could along the way.

MDF: Were you and your mother close?

Richard: Extremely. We had, and we still have, a very special bond. We're mother and son, and also best friends. She is as good as they come, and I missed her a great deal when I first went off to university.

MDF: Which university did you choose?

Richard: I was on scholarship at McMaster, actually. It was 1971. I'm exceptionally bright, much brighter, in fact, than my transcripts might indicate. I performed adequately in the public schools, enough to get my scholarship and enough to get chosen for several appearances on TV quiz shows, but I never threw myself into my studies completely and could have done even better had I really tried.

MDF: What did you study? What degree did you take?

Richard: I entered the independent studies program with an eye on Canadian lit, but I left in 1975 without taking my degree. I was only a few credits shy, but somehow I had no incentive to finish. I spent the next few years working at odd jobs, reading, and exploring various political groups and ideas. This was in Toronto.

MDF: How did you happen to find your way to the Craft?

Richard: It had everything to do with the death of my closest friend, in 1978. I was a Marxist and an atheist at the time, very radical politically, very disillusioned with the establishment, very materialistic in my outlook, a kind of cynical Communist. But when Dale was killed everything began to change. I was totally devastated, totally crushed by his death, and yet found I had no way, no *inner* way, to deal with it. I kept coming up against my materialist philosophy. I couldn't cry, couldn't mourn, couldn't even honor his memory. I felt sealed off within myself, like a prisoner. At the Catholic service an old friend of ours put his arms around me and whispered in my ear that Dale was with Jesus. What shit, I thought. Is that what people say to console themselves? Am I supposed to say that? Going home on the train I began to write poetry to the Goddess, to the power of life, to the great wheel of the year, the cycle of seasons. I had heard about the Goddess on and off for years and had read about matriarchy and the seasonal myths of the Greeks and Romans during high school and university, but I had never thought about it much and now for some reason it came pouring out of me. I began to realize that everything derived from the same creative female force and went back to it in the end. Death no longer seemed horrifying, empty, arbitrary, but part of a timeless pattern. I began to feel awkward and guilty about being an atheist. It suddenly seemed wrong, and blind, like a bitter stubbornness rather than a philosophical position. I wanted a spiritual life; I wanted spiritual fulfill-ment. I wanted to complete a part of myself that was there, alive, awake, and starving. And I felt the power of the Goddess, of the earth, of the female. I knew it in a way I had never known it before. I think women are strong, even though they don't have cocks. Male gods, Jesus and the others, don't make sense to me. Women are at the foundation of things, the very creation of the world, and they aren't cut off from their bodies and their feelings as men are. When I read *The Spiral Dance* in '79 I found not only many great ideas to add to my own thinking; I also found many of the ideas I had had on the train expressed beautifully. *This* made sense. This was a view that I could totally identify with. There is no doubt in my mind that *The Spiral Dance* is one of the best and most important books ever written. My spiritual crisis was resolved as I turned the pages, and by the end I was converted, in my own mind, to the Craft.

MDF: Could you be more specific about what it was in *The Spiral Dance* that really grabbed you?

Richard: The theology was true. The view of *everything* was true. The female is the dominant force and gender; the male is adjunctive to the female and subordinate. The book had it right. Also, the model of maleness that the book presented was one I could identify with. It wasn't an aggressive or destructive model; it didn't appear that way to *me,* and it didn't appear that way to women either, as I have discussed the subject with them. This book taught me that I didn't have to go around raping women to be a man, and I also didn't have to be castrated to be a feminist. I am a fully heterosexual male. I am manly, strong, and confident. You can see what I am just by talking to me, and I don't have to hurt others or be macho-patriarchal to prove anything.

MDF: Were there other themes in *The Spiral Dance* that intrigued you?

Richard: I was very taken with the ecological emphasis, and that, along with world peace, is still a huge part of my thinking. When I realized that Dale's death meant ultimately that he had reunited with the Goddess or the maternal power (to which we're all joined whether or not we know it), I also realized the earth had to be protected, kept whole and clean as an expression of the living Goddess. It seemed awful to think the very ground we get buried in could be poisoned with chemicals. This aspect of the book was very important to me. The more I read, and the more I discussed my ideas with Sarah [Richard's girlfriend at this time], the more I was convinced by the Craft's conception of things. Finally, I underwent my first possession, or trance, my first true mystical encounter.

MDF: Could you tell me about that? When did it occur? What was it like?

Richard: It was about one year after reading *The Spiral Dance.*

Sarah was withdrawing from me at the time. We were beginning to disagree on a number of things and I felt I was on my way to developing my own ideas, my own philosophy, apart from everyone else. I wanted my own connection with the Goddess, with the divine. Sarah did, too, and perhaps she sensed what I was going through, but I remember being alone that night and wanting to feel my own power, my own strength, by myself, with no one around and no one else's ideas in my head. I cast a circle, called in the directions, and chanted and danced for a while. I then began to feel another being taking over my body. I felt something moving my arms and legs. Something was expressing itself through my limbs. A few moments later it moved into my belly, so sharply and so forcefully that I grunted. My dancing began to stem from my belly, my center, the area directly behind my navel. This continued for perhaps ten minutes, until Bran appeared.

MDF: Bran?

Richard: The ancient Celtic fertility god. I had become acquainted with him through the literature but had never paid any particular attention. Yet here he was, directly present in my consciousness, a part of my mind. I knew instantly that my role on earth was to assist Him, to serve His cause. I am here to aid Bran, was my thought. The God is speaking through *me* to others. Not only did my atheism disappear once and for all, but my priesthood began. I bore Bran's message, and it was within *my* circle, cast by me, that my mission got underway. I wanted to go further with Witchcraft after this, to bring my experience to other Witches, and share my vocation with them, too. I began to attend Wiccan festivals, to participate in a coven in Toronto, and to deepen my spiritual life through reading and study. That's the big change. I now have a spiritual existence where before I had only my Marxist doctrines.

MDF: Why Bran? What do you think? You've read of a good many Goddesses and Gods.

Richard: I believe it is connected to my reading of Robert Bly. His poetry makes it very clear that we all have a wild man within, a kind of precivilized, untamed masculine power—very sexual, very masterful—and that most of us never manage to live fully in and through this aspect of our nature. It gets socialized out of us, pushed down. As I danced and chanted in my circle, I began to feel its presence; it came surging up in me, my masculine capacity and strength. I was in the process of breaking up with

Sarah at the time. It was clear that we were not going to make it, although the disengagement was slow for both of us. And suddenly Bran comes in and says to me: "Here is your manhood; here is your power; here is your mission." I was linked to the archetype and became the kind of Witch whose spiritual and philosophical roots reach back to that particular figure.

MDF: Were you initiated into the Craft immediately after Bran's visit?

Richard: No; not immediately after. When Sarah and I broke up, I decided to spend some time on a communal farm in southern Ontario; it was there that I met Pam and started the relationship that is currently going on. I needed a retreat to nature, a close communion with the earth, the plants, and animals. However, I eventually began to feel the need to return to the social world and the pressing issues of the day. I traveled to Buffalo with Pam, made contact with the Wiccan community, and in 1983 formally became a Witch. It was one of the biggest moments of my life, one of the big four, as I think of it. First there was Dale's death, then *The Spiral Dance,* then the appearance of Bran, and finally my initiation. My goals began to solidify. I knew I was a priest; I knew that I wanted communion with the divine, and I knew I wanted to work with and serve others, bring them to the world of Wicca. It's the fastest growing religion in the world because neither men nor women are satisfied with traditional faiths, traditional roles, traditional culture. All that stuff is in the process of destroying the earth, destroying Gaia [an ancient Greek earth mother], destroying the Goddess.

MDF: Do you regard the earth as a sentient, living organism?

Richard: Of course. How can anyone miss it? The Goddess exists *as* earth, and the earth exists *as* Goddess. We are part of Her, an expression of Her consciousness and being. The very atmosphere of the planet sustains us, nourishes us; it is part of a unified, coherent, living system. Everything works together at the physical and spiritual levels. We don't have to think of Her, strictly speaking, as *consciousness. We* are her thinking process; we are part of her total body. Our liver doesn't have to think; we think for it, take care of it, nourish it. Our liver isn't conscious in a definite way, but neither is it without consciousness as part of us. The world is a system, and the Goddess is interfused throughout the system as its foundation and organizing principle.

MDF: In my reading of Wiccan texts, including of course *The*

Spiral Dance, I've noticed that Witches are concerned with the use of power, particularly personal power. Could you tell me something about that?

Richard: Power is a *force,* a manifestation of the primal universe. It is out there, all around us. What has to be borne in mind is that we get power to give power, and then we get it *back* again from that to which we gave it, as Gardner [Gerald B. Gardner, a prominent modern Witch] points out. If I project power into the circle, it doesn't matter where it comes from. The circle becomes a portable temple because I project my power into it, but then I get power back from the circle as I invoke the Goddess and develop a particular ritual. It is give-and-take, a two-sided relation, a source and a receiver.

MDF: But do you have a particular strategy for getting power?

Richard: I *ask* for it. I ask the Goddess to bring it to me, from her domain or being, or if I feel it dwelling inside already, I just summon it up. It's a matter of changing awareness, or clicking in to it, or being open to it. There's no need to define it in that sense. It works, so why worry about it?

MDF: I gather that magical practice is an integral part of Witchcraft today. How, in your view, does magic work?

Richard: It has everything to do with power, with what I just told you. If I have a magical purpose to accomplish, I link my awareness to the power source and then send the power out to do the job. In my trances I may collaborate with specific outside forces of a divine nature, but I can't go into that. I don't mean to say I don't have my own inner sources of power, either. I have enormous energy, great power of my own, as everyone does, and it is through this, finally, that collaboration proceeds. I think of it in my own mind as producing the great vitality, the source of all magical accomplishments worldwide. I don't use wands; I don't use crystals. I rely upon the circle and my own powers of communion.

MDF: What about magical practice in the coven?

Richard: It works very much the same way. We cast the circle, we call in the directions, we light the candles, join hands, ask the Goddess and the Gods to be with us, and then we experience the influx of energy. We may chant, or dance, or meditate as we raise our cone [of power]. It is all very basic, very elemental, very raw in Bly's sense. We are naked, and we are in a place that is halfway between the world of the Goddess and the world of mortals. It is a place that is not a *place,* a time that is not a time. It is the center of the universe, a special kind of relativity, the circle that is all circles, and one. When we've sent our power to its goal, whatever that happens to be, then we celebrate with hugs and kisses. There is no hesitation or embarrassment. Wiccan men and women interact on a different plane. We are equal, spiritual, devoted in our eclectic pantheon. I like the mixed group, the men and the women together. Male groups don't work for me. I want both sexes present, both sexes participating, as they do in the natural order.

MDF: You mentioned directing power to its goal. What sort of goal did you mean?

Richard: We heal when we learn of someone who requires it. We stop logging where it shouldn't be going on. We stop the developers from turning farm land into shopping malls; we stop employers from excluding women from executive positions. We visualize the situation, we visualize the desired outcome, and we send the power to accomplish it. We may visualize a valley saved from the polluters and destroyers; a cancer patient cured of a malignancy; a difficult birth proceeding smoothly; or a politician changing his reactionary stand on an important social or environmental issue—all of this. For us, the divine is not static. It is our activity. The Wiccan crusade is a union of spiritual and political ends.

MDF: Will the coven you are organizing be meeting in the near future?

Richard: Pam and I have only been here [in Vancouver] a few months, and the organization of the coven is turning out to be a very slow process. I've asked Pam to be one of the participants but at this time she doesn't seem to be willing. She's continuing her study of Witchcraft, however, and I feel she'll eventually be initiated, and our children, too. I have a Pan-like influence on people; my power eventually gets to them. That's why I am referred to in so many Wiccan articles and books. People remember me.

MDF: Have you written books and articles yourself? May I read them? I am most eager.

Richard: I will write the books when the time comes. Right now my business is to organize the coven and to get involved in the Wiccan activity on the West Coast. It's a new life.

Mary

I met Mary at a vegetarian health food restaurant near downtown Vancouver on a weekend afternoon in the early spring of 1990. She was a stocky, greying woman of fifty, rather mannishly dressed in trousers and a plaid shirt. She had steel-rimmed glasses on, was businesslike and straightforward in her demeanor, a little impatient, and, as it turns out, very heavily involved in the organization and the activities of the Craft on the West Coast. Indeed, Mary might well be described as a Wiccan leader and spokesperson for the Portland-Seattle-Vancouver "triangle." After chatting briefly about her many social, political, and religious interests, we began the interview.

MDF: Tell me a little bit about your background.

Mary: I was born in Philadelphia, the youngest of three children in a devoutly Catholic family. As a child I was expected to attend church services regularly, participate in the mass, go to Sunday school—the whole ball of wax. There was no arguing or reasoning with mom and dad on this score. I was Catholic, my family was Catholic, and that was that. As a teenager I experienced considerable anxiety in the face of my sexual feelings. I had a terrible time at confession with the probing questions of the priest, and lived in constant expectation of exposure, excommunication, and eventual hell-fires—the sort of thing James Joyce described so well in that book about his childhood in Ireland.

MDF: *Portrait of the Artist as a Young Man?*

Mary: That's the one; it was very much like that, what I went through as a kid, and I still haven't recovered entirely from it. I probably never will, in spite of constant work on myself, therapy, and even attending a kind of AA specifically designed to assist lapsed Catholics with a lifelong hangover from their childhoods. Sometimes, when I think about my involvement with Witchcraft, I say to myself, if mom and dad could see me now! I still expect them to walk in on me one day, look around at my Wiccan tools and associates, and collapse in horror and revulsion.

MDF: But at least you had a cohesive, close-knit family, right?

Mary: It sounds that way, but it really wasn't. My brother and sister were a lot older than me, and my dad died when I was eleven. I was more or less happy as a kid, but I remember feeling lonely and isolated much of the time. Mom was always working, struggling to make a few bucks, dad was gone, and I was shunted off to my grandparents much of the time, especially after school. They loved me I suppose, but they were very silent, withdrawn people and I spent many many hours wishing mom were there and feeling I was somehow in outer space, not entirely on the earth, in orbit or something. I think this poisoned my relation with my mother, over time. When I think of her now I don't have a clear, strong sense of her. She may also have had a bit of the martyr in her. She was often depressed, overworked, mostly on her own, without boyfriends or suitors: an Irish widow, down-in-the-mouth, joyless, bitter; working, sleeping, feeding her kids. It was pretty grim. By my late teens I think I hated everything and everyone around me, including Catholicism and all its trappings, but I still considered myself a Catholic, was loaded with guilt for my sinful thoughts, and was dying to get the hell out of my neighborhood and out of Philadelphia, which I did when I turned nineteen.

MDF: How did you find your way to the Craft?

Mary: It was a long process. I went to New York City after leaving home and tried to carve out a conventional life for myself. I trained as a salesperson, a secretary, an airline hostess, but ultimately felt empty and lost. So I moved to the Village and began to interact with people who had alternate political and religious views. At twenty-four I found myself pregnant, and terrified at the thought of my mother finding out. I moved to San Francisco and spent the sixties raising my son, working at various jobs and trying to find my way toward a philosophy and a life-style that would give me a feeling of fulfillment. I was dogged by loneliness and by a sense of disconnection. When I came to Canada in 1971, I was like a fallow field waiting for a spiritual seed. It was planted a few years later when I met Merlin Stone [an influential feminist author]. She didn't talk about Witchcraft but she talked a good deal about the Goddess and I began to glimpse a religious conception of things that would be meaningful to me.

MDF: When did you actually become a Witch?

Mary: It was 1978. I was living in the interior of British Columbia and was deeply involved in women's issues. Several of my associates convinced me that I was more needed in Vancouver, and so I moved to the east side and got involved in assisting homeless and battered women. After three or four months, I met a local artist who was also a Witch and who invited me, along with three other women, to participate in a full moon ritual at Jericho Beach. Carol was a very big woman with a great sense of humor, sparkling clear eyes, and an unforgettable cackling laugh. She wore brightly colored skirts and blouses, lots of heavy costume jewelry, and had her dark red hair piled way up high and full of shiny, studded combs and pins. When we got to the beach it was nearly 1:00 and there was no one around. The night was clear, with the full moon on the water and a feeling of magic in the air. I was ready for anything, but I must admit I was astounded at the power of the rite and at the depth of the change it created in me. It was the circle that did it. As soon as it was drawn in the sand and I stepped into it, I knew that something of great significance was about to occur and that I would never be the same again. If I had to indicate exactly how I felt I would say that I had the sensation of finally coming home after a long and stressful absence. The loneliness I was so used to vanished. I was somewhere. I belonged. I was no longer in orbit. And when we joined hands, that sensation was hugely enhanced. I wasn't simply in a circle, but in a circle of *women*. I could feel the ancient sisterhood, the tradition, thousands of years old. It was as if patriarchy had denied me my sense of identity and selfhood. I knew deep inside that my experience was both personal and political, and that what was occurring had social as well as religious meaning.

MDF: Can you tell me more about what happened that night?

Mary: We sat on the sand and chanted together, hands joined. After a few minutes I began to feel the earth beneath me awaken, come to life, and respond to my sense of connection. As I looked at my feet, I spied a cord emerging from their palms, between the ball and the heel. It was a slimy, shiny, rope-like cord but made of a living substance, like flesh, or the skin of a sausage. It was boring down into the earth, slowly, steadily, and apparently with no end. When the chanting stopped—it may have been twenty minutes later—the cord just faded away, dissolved into the blackness, but the feeling of connection remained. I felt close to the women who were with me, and somehow deeply and permanently joined to the earth. As it turns out, I organized a coven a few weeks later (after having been initiated into the Craft), and two of the women who were with me that night became coven members. This was several years ago, and we're still together today, meeting regularly at my home.

MDF: You experienced a powerful contact with the earth that night. Do you regard the earth as an organism, a sentient, cohesive creature?

Mary: The earth is the Goddess and the Goddess is the earth. They are indistinguishable at the level of spiritual apprehension. My awareness of the earth is answered by the earth's awareness of me. I regard my way of life, my involvement with Witchcraft, my attempt to make known the truths of the ancient religion, as itself an expression of the earth and of the Goddess whose power originally infused the planet with many levels of awareness, including, of course, the spiritual level. For me, to say Goddess is to say consciousness, awareness; and to say consciousness, awareness is to express an earthly event, a daily happening on and of the planet. People, of course, have many aspects, and I regard all of them as expressions of the Goddess, expressions that often receive metaphorical representation through a variety of deities— many Goddesses representing many facets of ourselves, but all Goddesses when taken together are ultimately Goddess, one. The Wiccan concern with the desecration of the earth, pollution, the cutting down of forests, the whole ecological mess has to be seen from this spiritual angle as well as from a practical angle. Our pollution is finally a transgression, a wounding of a precious body, a kind of slow crucifixion, but this time the god is female, and the god is *ourselves*. We are part of the agony, part of the death. It is not so much a destruction as a self-destruction. As we come to realize this more and more through Witchcraft, the screams of the planet-body get louder and more distinct. Maybe everyone will hear them, eventually. If things go really well people will realize that the word Goddess itself imposes a limitation on understanding, that it can mean a female version of God. This is, of course, wrong. The Goddess is the beginning, derived from no one and from nothing, the creation of the universe itself. But at the moment it seems "Goddess" is the best we can do.

MDF: The literature of the Craft refers frequently to power, and to its connection with magic. What are your views on this score?

Mary: Power resides within the individual as a gift of life, or life-energy. It also resides in the surrounding universe. Some individuals have more of it than others, some less, some very little. In addition, some people are able to draw it from the world around them in a remarkable way; those are the ones who are capable of magical activities. To use power, to accomplish a magical purpose, one must learn to *focus,* to direct energy through concentration and visualization. For example, if I am about to purchase a car and if I want the salesperson to lower the price by 10 percent, I must visualize him, or her, doing this—concentrate on it. If I am able to mobilize sufficient power and to direct it effectively, I will achieve my end. The same holds for group action, for the coven. Power can be raised and directed in great concentrations for a number of purposes, including the betterment of society. But what is most striking about power and its relation to people is the *waste* of it. People don't realize what they might accomplish through this technique, what great changes they might bring about, and so the world goes on and on in its sorry condition, getting worse each day.

MDF: Do you feel your involvement in Witchcraft has increased your power?

Mary: Without a doubt, especially when I enter the circle. I may not have been *reborn* that night on the beach but I came very close to what that must be like. I gained a new existence, and I do believe in the possibility of rebirth for all people no matter how badly the past has damaged them. But the Craft not only enlarged my power, it clarified for me the way I should be using it, where I should be sending my energy. At the moment, I admit, I am in a sort of stagnant condition. My power comes and goes, and right now it's at a low point. I expect more power soon [laughing].

MDF: To what purpose will you put it?

Mary: Witchcraft today is more than a religion; it's a political statement about women, and about the environment. I want to see the word Witch reclaimed. I want to see the Craft making positive changes in the world, in attitudes toward and treatment of women (and other minorities such as native Indians); I want to see the Craft helping to turn around our present wasteful and destructive treatment of the planet, its resources and beauties. Witchcraft is a combination of the political and the spiritual, and I want to use my power to fulfill both these aspects of it. Most of all, I mean to do more in assisting the battered and the homeless. Remember, I work with street people much of the time and need all the power I can muster to do that effectively. My old Catholic values may have something to do with this involvement, but it is more than that, too. I am, after all, a triple Aquarian.

MDF: If you had to express the essence of Witchcraft in one sentence, what would that sentence be?

Mary: I'd specify first that I was speaking of white Witchcraft, or the modern Witchcraft movement; then I would say, Witchcraft is the art of directing power to accomplish a variety of worthy aims, both spiritual and material in nature. We mean business.

At a Coven Meeting

We gathered in the living room of a character home situated on Vancouver's east side at 7:30 in the evening during the spring of 1990. The room was large, with a highly polished hardwood floor from which two or three oriental rugs had been removed and piled in one corner. On the mantel about the unlit fireplace were several antique statuettes of female deities, and several large, luminescent pieces of crystal. The walls of the room were tastefully covered with a mauve paper highlighted by a sinuous floral pattern. A sofa and several high-backed chairs in the Victorian style had been circularly placed at the living room's periphery, and at the center of the hardwood floor stood four large candles and holders arranged rectangularly, a bowl of clear water, a saucer of salt, and a large, blue canvas bag tied at the top and resembling a hiking pack. In the adjoining dining room a good-sized oak table had been laid with plates of fruit, vegetables, and cheese, and with two large pitchers of what turned out to be apple juice. There were no lights on in the living room which was illuminated by the chandelier in the dining area. All nine members of the coven (seven women, two men) had been informed in advance of my participation. As people arrived, they sat or stood about chatting and smiling. By 7:50 P.M. attendance was complete and the meeting began.

The Grounding

At the suggestion of the Priestess, a tall, fair, middle-aged woman attired in a floor-length white gown, we formed a circle in the living room, standing with hands joined. After a silence of perhaps two minutes, the exercise in grounding commenced as follows: We were told, first, to extend our arms upward toward the sky and to visualize the clouds, the moon, the stars, and the galaxies, all of which were "manifestations of the Goddess."[5] We were then told to imagine an opening in the tops of our heads into which we were to pull "the power of the cosmos." After four or five minutes of what the Priestess called "reaching for the sky," we were asked to sit, again in a circle but with hands disjoined, and to visualize our "roots," which emerged from our abdominal or genital areas, extending themselves into the ground. More specifically, we were asked to visualize these "roots" discovering their way into the earth's "crystals, or caves, or mud, or into the bones of the dead." All of this was suggested by the Priestess in a firm, yet soothing tone: "ground and center." As we focused, as we pushed our roots into the planet, the Priestess asked us to join hands and continue with the grounding. We were, in her words, "reaching together to the center of the earth" for "power," for "fresh energy." We were also "dumping" our egotic preoccupations and petty problems into the world's "hot center" where they would evaporate, thus leaving our "souls" in a "cleansed" condition. As the group's effort proceeded, one member began to rock back and forth and chant. The others seemed to be deeply absorbed in thought or in meditative states. This continued for perhaps ten minutes, at which point the Priestess slowly rose, and the members of the circle rose with her. Smiles were exchanged at this juncture, and lots of eye contact was initiated. People stretched their necks and shoulders, moved their hips, breathed deeply, and shared a brief remark or giggle. Shortly thereafter, the Priestess requested us to sit again and suggested that Peter begin to call in the directions.

The Directions, the Circle, and the Ablutions

Employing a copy of *The Spiral Dance*,[6] which had somehow appeared, Peter, a young, red-bearded man in floppy, blue cotton pants and a kind of loose-fitting Mexican shirt, read aloud:

> Hail, Guardians of the Watchtowers of the South, Powers of fire, We invoke you and call you, Red lion of the noon heat, Flaming One! . . . Be here now! (56)

As Peter recited, the Priestess rose, and, with a pearl-handled knife that sported a blade of perhaps eight inches, made a semi-circular motion in the air. At the conclusion of his recitation, Peter lit one of the candles at the center of the hardwood floor and handed *The Spiral Dance* to another coven member (female) who had been designated by the Priestess a few seconds earlier. The new reciter intoned as follows:

> Hail, Guardians of the Watchtowers of the West, Powers of Water, We invoke you and call you, Serpent of the watery abyss, Rainmaker, Gray-robed twilight, Evening star! . . . Be here now!

Once again this was orchestrated with the Priestess' circular motions, and concluded with the lighting of a candle. After the final two directions were "called in" in a similar manner, the Priestess stepped outside the circle of seated bodies, and, with her knife pointed downward, walked once around the group to her original position, announcing, "The circle is cast. We are between the worlds, beyond the bounds of time, where night and day, joy and sorrow, meet as one." She then entered the circle's center and placed her knife on the floor next to the blue canvas bag. She took up the salt, poured it into the water, returned to her place with the bowl, sat down, and uttered a few sentences the gist of which was a request for purification through the Goddess. After touching the salted water to her hands, arms, and forehead, she passed the bowl to the members of the coven, each of whom repeated her ministrations and the last of whom returned the bowl to the center, next to the knife, bag, and candles.

The Goddess Comes

After members had been sitting quietly in the circle for two or three minutes, Sarah, a heavy-set, blond, bespectacled woman of perhaps thirty-five, dressed in jeans and a black sweater, suggested that we "call in the Goddess." I was startled a few seconds later to hear the coven members begin to chant, call, and sing most energetically on an individual basis. I am not certain who commenced the din (it was not the Priestess), but it continued for at least five minutes. I recorded the names of various deities including Isis, Diana, Hathor, Maat, Istar, Eros, and Nabu, as well as the names of several of the coveners. Apparently, some were calling to the Goddess by calling to each other, or to themselves. Toward the conclusion of this remarkable outburst, members began to pause and look at one another, squeeze each other's hands, grin, laugh, and embrace with remarks such as, "She's here!" and "She's come!" and with questions such as, "Can you feel Her presence?" and "Is she with you too?" When the man seated next to me (Charles) asked me whether I could sense the Goddess' presence, I smiled at him warmly, then looked away.

As the commotion gradually died down, the group began to focus its attention on the Priestess who announced the evening's work. In a serious, low voice she told us that one of the coven members, Stephanie, had been recently and unexpectedly diagnosed as diabetic. Obliged to inject herself three times a day with insulin and to live with an uncertain future, Stephanie was presently undergoing a severe depression. Members listened intently to the Priestess and then turned to Stephanie with expressions of commiseration and concern. A tiny woman barely five feet and ninety pounds with short black hair, a pronounced aquiline nose, and pearl, horn-rim glasses, Stephanie smiled softly at her fellow coveners and seemed on the verge of tears. When the soothing and commiseration declined, Peter undertook what I quickly discovered to be a healing chant. He asked the Goddess to touch Stephanie with Her healing powers. As Peter chanted, the members of the coven rocked, swayed, and chanted softly with him until another chant began, this time from Sarah. Hers, I later found out, was a "water chant" also designed to pacify and heal the "patient." Again the group swayed and rocked and chanted softly to themselves.

As it turns out, however, all this chanting had a crucial, additional purpose, namely to "raise power" for the central rite which got underway when the Priestess rose, went over to Stephanie, assisted her to her feet, and began to undress her. Stephanie was wearing a long, black cotton dress that was loosely fitted and that was simply lifted over her head after she had removed her flat, canvas walking shoes. She did not have a brassiere on, and after her dress was laid neatly to one side, she removed her underwear. Naked, she was led to the circle's center which had been quickly cleared of objects. The Priestess then lowered Stephanie gently to the floor where she lay flat on her back, her legs fully extended and her arms straight down at her sides. After staring at Stephanie intensely for a moment or two and then nodding with satisfaction, the Priestess took up the blue canvas bag, removed its tie, and reached inside.

Her hand returned with a smooth, flat, circular stone about the size of a small tea saucer. She handed this stone to Peter and then reached in for another which she handed to me. A few minutes later the bag was empty and each member of the circle had in his possession three stones. Leaning down to Stephanie, the Priestess placed two stones on her upper chest and another between her breasts. Following suit, coven members, including the writer, placed stones on different parts of Stephanie's anatomy until she was virtually covered with them; they rested on her legs, her arms, her belly, her pubis, and her forehead as she lay flat and still. There was no talking during all of this, and no flinching on Stephanie's part when a stone tumbled off her calf and had to be replaced.

Then, for perhaps ten full minutes, in complete silence, the group focused its "power" on Stephanie's stone-covered body. The aim, of course, was to heal her through an enormous concentration of energy and with the aid of the stones, laden as they were with the natural force of the Goddess. The ritual as a whole, I was subsequently told, was designed also to call up the "patient's" own "healing powers." The group, in other words, was helping Stephanie to help herself. Thus, at the center of the magic circle and naked as a newborn babe beneath her blanket of maternal stones, Stephanie basked in the glow of the group's collective *wish* that she get better.

A faint stirring in the room marked the close of the focusing and wishing. The Priestess rose, went to the dining area, and returned with a cotton blanket. She knelt by Stephanie, removed the stones (which coven members quickly put back into the bag), and covered her up. At this point, everyone converged on Stephanie with smiles and soft, soothing words. They stroked her hair, arms, and shoulders, whispering congratulations. After smiling back and occasionally touching the faces of her fellow Witches, Stephanie began to speak from a benign, peaceful, inward place: "Thank you," she said over and over again; "my god, I feel so wonderful!" "I love you!" "This is unbelievable!" A few moments later she got up, donned her underwear and dress, and rejoined the circle that had newly reestablished itself with members holding hands and with the Priestess in her commanding position.

For five minutes or so everyone chatted, laughed, smiled, relaxed, and remarked on what had just occurred. "It was great!" "I felt so much!" "She's going to get better!" "Did you feel the *power*?" "The Goddess was here!" When the group's attention finally shifted back to the Priestess, she asked, after a moment of complete silence, "Shall we say goodbye to the Goddess?" There was a quick, general assent followed by individual farewells on the part of coven members who began to chant, sway, and sing. I recorded: "Kali, thank you for being here"; "Stay if you will, go if you must"; "I will keep you, I will keep you, I will keep you" (this from Peter). A few moments later, the same people who had called in the directions bid them adieu with, for example, "Farewell, power of the North who brought to us the strength of the healing earth," and, "Farewell, power of the West who bathed us with the waters of spiritual rebirth." This time, however, *The Spiral Dance* did not appear to direct the verbalizations of the ritual. Finally, when the last direction had been addressed and the last candle snuffed, the Priestess rose and pronounced, "The circle is open but unbroken. Blessed be." A feeling of solemnity and success was clearly in the air at this point, as if nothing could compare with the wonderful healing of Stephanie that had just occurred. With the Priestess' final blessing, the smiling and chatting coven members arose and moved to the dining area to partake of the food and drink. As people munched and milled around between the two rooms, Sarah said loudly, "may you never hunger or thirst!" Those closest to her nodded and smiled affirmatively; others paid no attention. The socializing continued for perhaps thirty minutes amidst talk of the next meeting, the distribution of notices and newsletters, and frequent salutations to Stephanie, who seemed very much restored. As departing coven members made their way to the front door, the Priestess was on hand to exchange a final word or two with them. To me she said soberly although not unpleasantly, "let us know if you wish to join our circle again."

4

Bewitchment Everywhere: The Ubiquity of the Separation/Union Conflict

A single, overriding purpose informs this concluding chapter: I want to disclose the extent to which the separation/union conflict that governs the underlying motivations of modern Witchcraft may discover its way into a variety of pursuits that we regard as more or less normal expressions of human behavior in culture. I want to reveal the degree to which many of our most customary, taken-for granted activities such as working to get rich, or becoming involved in the sciences, or expressing one's devotion to country or party may harbor what we can term an element of witchery. I say "element" to make it perfectly clear that I do not mean to place an equal sign between the aforementioned activities and the practice of Witchcraft.[1] Obviously there are gigantic differences between cherishing an ideology, pursuing scientific truth, seeking after gold, and worshipping the Goddess. But there may also be crucial similarities, and it is these that I want to explore. Why? To what end? Purely and simply to increase our understanding of what we are doing on the planet, and, through that, to enhance our ability to make our conduct less compulsive, less *driven*. Just on the face of it, the separation/union conflict, as described by Mahler and as evinced by the Wiccan movement, must be very confusing to a good many human beings at *some* level of their experience; that is, to move psychically and emotionally *away* from objects in a manner that also signifies unconsciously moving *toward* them, to choose substitutes that imply separation and *at the same time* promise reunion—in short, to go forward and backward simultaneously must surely constitute one of the most obfuscating and potentially frustrating aspects of our psychological existence. It may be of value, I believe, to shed a bit of light on this, to gain some distance from it. Take, for example, that bewitching stuff we call money.

The Religio-Economic Realm

Silvio Gesell (1958, 32) declares in his classic study *The Natural Economic Order* that "goods, not money, are the real foundation of economic life"; he then asserts, "money is a means of *exchange* and nothing else." This is a pivotal assertion, one that can help us to understand not only the *transitional* nature of economic organization but the *transitional* nature of cultural organization as a whole—something we touched on earlier, in Chapter 2.

Of the transitional object itself Phyllis Greenacre (1971, 384) writes that it "represents not only the mother's breast and body but the total maternal environment as it experienced in combination with sensations from the infant's body." It serves as a "support and convoy" during the "period of rapid growth which necessitates increasing separation from the mother." It is a "protective escort," and its "softness and pliability" (if it happens to be a blanket or cloth) "are useful at a time when the infant's perceptions of the our world are changing and when speech is forming." Thus it "lends itself to symbolic representation and plays a role in promoting illusion by relating new experiences to earlier ones." Finally, it "consolidates the illusion of maternal supplementation." What I wish to stress immediately here is this: The creation and the use of the transitional object derive from the same psychological urge that lies behind the formation of symbols generally, that is, the compelling need to internalize the environment, to grip the external world, and thus to answer the dilemma of separation with the magic of dual-unity, or the condition of having the object in fantasy and relinquishing it in reality.

Now, when we realize that money is a powerful, complex *symbol,* that it is valued, in the words of Furnham and Lewis (1986, 48), "because it represents or is associated with various *desirable objects,*" we also realize that the *exchange* which money is fated to accomplish at the unconscious level will engage the entire separation-individuation problem. Where money is concerned "exchange" will focus directly the tension of the physical and psychological *boundaries* established by individuals and institutions, the whole "business" of "merging," "withdrawing," "taking over," "incorporating," "moving in"—the metaphors of the marketplace in all their underlying significance. Indeed, to "exchange" is to touch upon the very basis of human existence itself, in which Eros draws forth the sexual response between people during nature's essential "transaction," the one that leads to the exchange between the mother and the infant at her breast. To say that money is a means of "exchange" and "nothing else" is not simply true, it is *profoundly* true, true in a way that directs our attention to the deep, emotional life of the species. As for the *transitional* implications, they are clear enough: Money is a kind of transitional object triggering transitional aims. Its complex symbolism reaches down to crucial issues bound up with the crises of the early period, the crises which color all subsequent psychological experience.

That money is customarily associated with *food*, with *survival*, also harbors unconscious significance and touches upon the problems of union and separation—the *oral* problems that are forever tied to the maternal object and the breast. It is in the infant's relationship with the mother that psychoanalysis spies the origin of the "oceanic feeling," the feeling in which the *boundaries* between the self and other disappear, the feeling in which one exchanges himself for the other, or is indistinguishable from the other. That money is exchanged for food, is, in a sense, indistinguishable from food, not only links economics to psychology, particularly with regard to the mother-infant interaction, it also links economics and psychology to *religion,* and especially to religious "mysteries" in which ego boundaries disappear in the divine *exchange* between the individual and the God who is his sustenance, his food, his *wafer.* We are not dealing here simply in metaphor but in a metaphoric version of psychic reality. The "oceanic feeling" is grounded in the same bond in which religious feeling is grounded—the bond that overcomes separation.

As we noted again and again in our analysis of the rites of the Craft, religion strives to answer the discontents of anxiety, separation, isolation, and mortality through its particular method of reconstituting the parental tie. However, such discontents are also addressed and paradoxically deepened by the economic system (religion's ancient adversary) which works to compensate for the original loss of the object through *substitutes*—wealth, power, possession. In the development of Protestantism, the two—economics and religion—formed a joint assault on the infantile dilemma, an assault which constituted, at another level, a remarkable attempt to resolve the ancient conflict between God and gold. That conflict was not resolved, of course, because—and this is the point—the enemies, God and gold, are not really enemies at all but "brothers under the skin."

As Becker (1975, 77) reminds us in *Escape from Evil,* the power of God has always been present in the metal, direct support for which may be found in the *Upanishads* (1965) and countless other works where the face of God is concealed behind a circle of gold. The psychological meaning of all this is further expressed in religious ornament, and, most strikingly, in the Protestant attempt to *deny* the equivalency by stripping the churches, an attempt that was guiltily rooted in the lust for gold that characterized Protestant life. We begin to spy from this perspective the compulsive or obsessional ground of our economic organization, the discontent of our civilization from an economic angle. Proffering a version of the maternal object, promising a magical reunion with the breast, the economic order teases, even titillates, the unconscious requirements of millions of human beings, for the desired symbiosis is *actually over,* the longed-for mother is no longer *there.* In Freud's way of looking at it, because the "gold" *itself* is *not* an infantile wish, its possession cannot bring happiness (cf. Wiseman 1974, 49). In the deepest psychoanalytic sense, then, ordinary religion and ordinary economics are *one.* Money and the sacred meet in the need to retain the tie to the object, in the dynamics of internalization, and its subsequent projective creations. Not without transitional significance is the anthropologists' discovery that the first banks were temples, temples in which both money and sanctified food were stored (cf. Brown 1959, 246).

Money and the Magna Mater

Money's *oral* significance, its unconscious connection to the objects of the early period, has of late been disclosed in a psychoanalytic literature that for decades had been ruled by theories based on the "anal stage." The sacrificial bull, William Desmonde (1976, 125) informs us in terminology that strikingly recalls our discussion of modern Witchcraft, was "often regarded as a fertility spirit or embodiment of the crops emanating from the goddess Earth." Eating the bull "represented an eating of the goddess or mother image" and expressed a wish "to incorporate the mother," to recapture the "infantile state of nondifferentiation." It was the "acquisition of money" that admitted the bearer to the sacrificial feasts and that came to signify the discovery of a "mother substitute which provided an infallible source of emotional security." "Money," declares Desmonde, "originated in the obtaining and distributing of food, . . . symbolized mother's milk," and sparked "ideas and emotions connected to the breast." As for "participation in the communion symbolized by the early monetary forms," it denoted the "psychic attaining of identification with the mother image." Desmonde spies the paternal influence as he investigates "food rituals" which represent "the breaking through of irrational hostility toward the father" and which are closely associated with money's primitive uses, but that influence, he notes, is properly understood only when regarded in the light of its maternal antecedents. All of this, incidentally, is in accordance with the fact that, in Desmonde's words, "early coins were also amulets, magical devices for retaining the feeling of omnipotence associated with the oral stage." A. C. Haddon (1963, 25), in a nonpsychoanalytic survey of primitive money, calls such amulet-coins the "givers of life" in the ancient world.

Roheim (1976, 153), who strives to demonstrate that individual economic systems reflect the tensions in the familial organization of particular cultures, maintains that the very concept of property, or the internalization of a part of the external world into the self, "is tantamount to an erotic tie." For Roheim the basic psychoanalytic meanings in the whole area of possession and economic organization are to be discovered in the "curious connection between birth and property, between landed property and the mother's body." The "totemistic phase" of primitive society, which stands behind Freud's view of "civilization," has ultimately a *projective* import. It says, "Mother earth belongs to the ancestors, that is, the mother belongs to the father." The fundamental significance is maternal.

Similar items are underscored in Erikson's (1987, 512) classic study of the Yuroks, subsequently amplified by Posinsky. The Yuroks are constantly praying for money, not merely because it assists them in creating a ritual atmosphere, but because of what it establishes about them in their own and others' eyes. The possessor of money (in the form of shells) is one who is favored by nature and in particular by the Klamath river, the sacred source of life. Money means communal acceptance, good body contents, and above all, a full mouth. Posinsky (1976, 188) declares in this regard, "on a pre-Oedipal level the shell money is certainly equivalent to a positive introject, or 'good body contents'; but it also develops a phallic component which reinforces the previous ones." Thus to be poor originally means "to be hungry or empty," but it also comes to mean "to be without a penis."

There is a danger in emptiness *and also* in fullness. The latter derives from the projection of oral aggression onto the parents, and from the "ambivalence involved in fulness" which signifies *both* good and bad body contents. The fear of emptiness makes the Yuroks "greedy and retentive"; the fear of fullness makes them "moderate eaters who must keep the alimentary passage open." The resulting personality is "remarkably akin to a compulsion neurosis." In this way, the "men" of Yurok society are "perpetually involved in Oedipal rivalries," the "never-ending struggle for wealth and prestige."

Such findings call to mind Reich's (1949, 90) observation that money and the size of the penis are often equated in the unconscious. Lots of money equals a large penis. But this particular equation has ultimately a transitional significance. When one is feeling insecure, anxious, empty, one seeks support, emotive nourishment, or narcissistic supplies in the magical surrogate which actually possesses the power to provide supplies and nourishment in the "real world" and thus comes to be unconsciously associated with the internal system. One is held by money, reassured by money, made secure by money, and this security reaches "up" from the mother to those later "oedipal rivalries − " involving the father and siblings. As Roheim (1969, 264) expresses it, "castration anxiety" is ultimately related to the "absence of the mother"; the penis is ultimately a "means of reunion." Thus money, like the penis, is a way back to the object. Even as a source of food it has unconscious meaning, for as Roheim (1969, 181) points out, "the whole process of food distribution—or of wealth or success—is fraught with anxiety." The chief or emperor is sacred because he dispenses food, a function that connects him to God, the provider, on the one hand, and to God's intermediary, the priest, on the other. When medieval Byzantine monarchs, who were *both* sacred and secular rulers, impressed important visitors by showing them "whole roomfuls" of money, they created the impression, writes Michael Hendy (1985, 272) that "between God and the emperor there was no great difference." At the deepest psychoanalytic level, then, money, as a means of providing food, becomes associated with the entire maternal function, with sustenance, with acceptance, with protection. As for the power of money, it is measured in inner as well as in outer terms that correspond precisely with the context. The powerful, the rich, are *secure,* secure in the tie to the inner realm and in the "reality" which is a projective outgrowth of that tie. Hence, "to distribute things, to feed people, is to be a good mother" (Roheim 1969, 288).

Again and again Roheim (1969, 268) stresses the crucial connection between money and the tie to the object, particularly with regard to the central problem of power, or control. "Money gives one control over others, and that is what really tells the story. A lien upon another person means that you can at your will convert him into a giver. The inability to control the mother was the most crucial defeat of childhood." To anticipate a thesis, both the power in money generally, and the power-seeking of capitalist life in particular, are related to this preoedipal conflict. The wish is for power that magically fulfills the infantile need to control the maternal figure and her later derivatives. In the language of Witchcraft, the attainment of wealth or the possession of money means at the unconscious level the ability to "rule the circle."

As for the power of the penis and the power of capital, they are also connected thus; both are ways to the object, both are used transitionally to compensate for the crucial defeat of childhood. Stinginess and the compulsive desire for money answer "oral frustrations . . . riches and mother are magically identical . . . to be rich means to be full of good body contents" (Roheim 1969, 275). In this way, the drive for wealth is closely bound up with the unconscious drive for omnipotence. The "cornerstone of the urge to possess," writes Bergler (1954, 6), "is a compensatory mechanism the purpose of which is to heal a wound to the child's self-love, his narcissism," and the basic wound, the wound that catalyzes the formation of symbols in an effort to internalize the maternal object and thus discover her presence in *other* objects, is separation-in-the-widest-sense, both actual separation and the "fantastic" separation that surrounds the existence of the bad (not-to-be-controlled) object. Money "denies dependence," Bergler observes (1959, 6, 9), and "stabilizes feelings of rejection." It is a "blind for existing and repressed infantile conflicts." But as money is also bound up with religious ceremony, and particular with the practice of *sacrifice*, we had better take a moment to spy further connections between religion and the monetary world.

The Sacrificial Way to the Object

Hubert and Mauss (1964, 9) point out in their definitive study, first, that "sacrifice always implies a consecration; in every sacrifice an object passes from the common into the religious domain; it is consecrated." Second, the consecration "extends beyond the thing consecrated; among other objects, it touches the moral person who bears the *expenses* of the ceremony. The devotee who provides the victim which is the object of the consecration is not, at the completion of the operation the same as he was at the beginning." He has "acquired a religious character."[2] This acquiring of a religious character, this transformation of the devotee, brings into view the central aim of sacrificial behaviors:

> The thing consecrated serves as an intermediary between the sacrificer, or the object which is to receive the practical benefits of the sacrifice, and the divinity to whom the sacrifice is usually addressed. Man and the god are not in direct contact. In this way, sacrifice is distinguished from most of the fact grouped under the heading of blood covenant, in which by the exchange of blood a direct fusion of human and divine life is brought about. (S, 11)

Thus the chief purpose of sacrifice, which is rooted in an act of "exchange"—the very word Gesell uses to express the chief purpose of money—is *to establish a tie*, a *connection*, a *bond*, between the individual who feels the need for such a tie and the divinity to whom he directs his need. In psychoanalytic terms, that divinity is a projective version of the internalized object, a creation which springs from the individual's inner world where an absorption into the bad presence and its derivatives is underway. No longer sure of his inner bearings, experiencing a divisiveness, a self-alienation, a "guilt" that grows as the war between introjections heats up, the devotee seeks to find the good object again and thus to strengthen his internal boundaries by altering the areas in which exchange is occurring. It is not simply the security of the father's good graces that is sought but a deeper security which resides in the deeper layers of personality formation associated with the object of the early time. Hubert and Mauss' description would be both anthropologically *and* psychoanalytically correct were they to write not of the "fusion" of "human and divine life" that sacrifice strives to bring about but of the *refusion* that it seeks.

As for the animal (or "matter") used in the sacrificial action, it is either a "pure" or "sinless" victim, that is, 1) "clean" material offered the divinity in expiation for transgressions committed and designed to facilitate the cleansing of the devotee through his oral or manual touching, or 2) a "tainted" animal, one which through the ministrations of the priest bears away the sinfulness of the devotee so as to leave him in a cleansed or pure condition in God's eyes (*S*, 28–45). This is, of course, a condensation of much material in Hubert and Mauss and leaves out numerous customs and rites. It requires little psychoanalytic knowledge, however, to recognize that the split nature of the victim is a reflection of the split nature of the inner world, forged in the dynamics of internalization. The victim, like the god, is either a version of the good object and its derivatives or the bad object and its derivatives. The tension surrounding the victim reflects the tension which accrues in the ambivalent relationship to the object of the early time whose basic threat is loss, abandonment, rejection, separation. Yet the matter does not end here. So prevalent is this anxiety in infancy that it often gives rise to the fear of engulfment, that is, absorption into the bad object. Thus the sacrificial animal may actually become in the logic of the unconscious a *version of the divinity itself*. The internalized object of infancy is explicitly involved in the projective mechanisms which subsequently handle the conflicts arising from the inner world. In the magic of sacrifice the devotee is offered a safe or "sublimated" avenue to the fulfillment of his incorporative aims. Victim and god are *one* (Christ as lamb).

When Roy Schafer (1968, Chap. 8) calls the internalizations of infancy "immortal," he suggests the connection between *that* immortality and the "immortality of the gods." Both are immortal because the transitional aim, the transitional mode of existence, continues throughout life. As Hubert and Mauss express it, "the notion of sacrifice *to* the god developed parallel with that of sacrifice *of* the god" (*S*, 990). Gods do not simply "live" on the substances offered them, they "are born" by them (*S*, 91). The sacrificial substance bears a relation to the life-giving body, and particularly the breast, of life's first object, upon whom the life of the individual depends entirely, just as the inner or even actual life of the sacrificer depends on the refusion with the divinity to whom he addresses himself. When Hubert and Mauss tell us that sacrifice is at the deep psychological level a "guarantee against annihilation" (*S*, 64), they call to mind the annihilation experienced by the infant during periods of separation from, or loss of, the object, and during those periods when he confronts the bad object (often his own "bad" impulses), periods which are also a kind of separation or rejection. The fear of annihilation begins at the beginning and is inextricably bound up with separation from mother at birth and with the inevitable ambivalence of early object relations. Religious and particularly sacrificial activities are employed to cope with that ambivalence, to reestablish equilibrium on the inside and thus preserve order on the outside. One is permitted to indulge his ambivalence in his killing and eating of the victim (scapegoat), yet one is also able to reunite with the good object who, in the magic of the action and through the ministrations of the Priest, will accept one's forbidden desires and judge one "good." Sacrifice enables our repressions, especially repressions of aims associated with the earliest internalizations, to remain flexible and thus preserves social stability by keeping people in contact with their good objects, by making people psychically comfortable in the unity of the dual-unity situation.

Sacrifice, say Hubert and Mauss in words that bring the Wiccan literature to mind, "cuts the individual off from the common life, and introduces him step by step into the sacred world of the gods" (S, 22). This sacred or magical world into which the individual steps is a "fantastic" version of the "good" world of one's infancy, and its very existence expresses the human need for that good place, for the satisfaction and security which comes at the good breast, and in the body of the good object and her derivatives, the good father, the bosom of Abraham, the protector generally. That which the individual experiences in the "sacred world" is closely related to the "oceanic" experience of union, the "mystical" sense of harmony, merger, well-being which is fundamental to a large area of religious life and feeling.

Sacred Lucre

That money plays a central role in sacrificial activity gets not only at the transitional significance of money's complex symbolism but at the extent to which an economic system devoted to the acquisition of money can express transitional aims, can reflect the requirements and purposes of the religious system which is ostensibly at odds with the worldly order. That money is inextricably linked in its origin and function to primitive religion and in particular to primitive sacrifice has been indisputably established in the literature and does not require lengthy exposition. Everywhere in primitive culture, writes Einzig (1951, 72), the "sacred" character of money is apparent, as is its role in sacrificial activity.[3] If goods come from god and if money gets goods, then money is an integral aspect of god's giving or provision. This insight comes to the members of the group as the emotive aims of sacrifice are accomplished, aims bound up with the "immortal objects" of the inner world. While Max Weber (1958) is correct to suggest that in Protestantism the amassing of wealth, the total concentration upon riches, came to be a way of reaching God and thus, in our terms, a transitional phenomenon with an obsessive or even hysterical cast, money as a link to god has been there from the beginning; and in the characteristic ambivalence of the human animal toward his projected internalizations, money as the bad object, as filth, has also been there from the beginning, perhaps as a reaction-formation to the deep-seated need for (and fear of) merger.

What constituted the sacrificial animal in Protestantism, the animal offered the deity as the compulsive concentration on work and wealth went forward? What but the body of the Protestant himself, his own body, his own senses? As Weber (1958, 53) expresses it, "something more than mere garnishing for purely egocentric motives is involved. In fact, the *summum bonum* of this ethic, the earning of more and more money, combined with the strict avoidance of all spontaneous enjoyment of life, is above all completely devoid of any hedonistic admixture. It is thought of so purely as an end in itself, that from the point of view of the happiness of, or utility to, the single individual, it appears entirely transcendental and absolutely irrational. Man is dominated by the making of money, by acquisition as the ultimate purpose of his life." One's own physical organism, one's own sensuous animal, is rendered up in the magical attempt to reach the transitional god, the sacred lucre.

The psychodynamics of this neurotic behavior emerge more vividly when we recall with Einzig that the word for money in many primitive societies is similar to or even identical with the word *taboo* (*PM,* 72) which means, of course, forbidden or sacred or power-filled or awesome, usually in some religious context. What is desired and pursued is also perceived as dangerous, as reflecting a questionable aim, which focuses from still another angle the ambivalence bound up with the pursuit of wealth, with sacrifice, with religion, and with the internalized objects that are projectively employed as the foundation of these cultural activities. In some areas of the Pacific, *tambu* or money can still be offered the gods in expiation for transgression (*PM,* 72). In ancient Athens money "belonged to" or derived from the mother of the city herself; Athena and her owl are everywhere stamped on the coinage. Rings, too, were frequently used as money in ancient times (*PM,* 191), and rings are obviously bound up with key transitional phenomena, namely bonding, union, marriage, the sealing of contracts, especially with the paternal or maternal substitute.[4] One is "struck," Einzig remarks, "by the frequent association between primitive money and primitive religion." In many communities the "creation of money is attributed to supernatural powers" (*PM*, 370), for primitive man was guided largely by "religious concerns," and the "evolution of the economic system was itself largely influenced by the religious factor," in particular by the requirements for "sacrifice" (*PM*, 371).

Focusing for us again the transitional significance in Gesell's term "exchange," as well as the transitional significance of sacrificial conduct generally, Einzig writes in an unforgettable expression that "making sacrifice" to the "deity" is "a form of barter between man and his gods" (*PM*, 371). Not only the sacrificial animal but the very objects employed in the sacrificial action, the knife, the axe, the tripod, the cauldron, the spit (think of the Witch's tools) come to be used as money among primitive peoples. Such items created a "unit of account" (*PM*, 73) and might even be *exchanged* for a sacred beast. As for the payment of the priest, it, too, has clear transitional implications in that the priest is instrumental in establishing the tie between the individual and his god. Today, as the "plate is passed" in church, or metaphorically on television, we recognize how solidly this transitional use of money is established in our own society. One pays, and *then* one gets the good feeling, the sense of connection with and praise from the good object on the inside. As religion evolves, Einzig tells us, "donations to the gods" in the form of "precious metals" (*PM*, 373) become an integral aspect of spiritual life, a traditional part of that "sacrifice" of one's property ("let's all make a sacrifice today") which connects one, or *re*connects one, with the projective creations of the inner world, with the "divine."

It is interesting in this regard to note the current economic tendency toward the creation of what the experts call "pure money," that is to say, money "in which the medium of exchange function hardly exists" (Crump 1971, 189). In the words of Walter Neale (1977, 14, 16, 57), "the bulk of modern money—the demand deposits in banks—is not a thing, not a stuff at all, but a set of legally binding statements about rights and obligations. A demand deposit is a promise by the bank to pay the depositor or whomever the depositor orders the bank to pay." Money becomes "disassociated from physical things," and a matter of "promises, promises, nothing but promises." What could be more perfectly designed to engage the world of internalized objects, and in particular, the entire dual-unity situation! One's power, one's control, one's sacred *promise* of reunion, comes not only from the "impure" money in one's pocket but from the "pure" variety that is both present and absent, linked to one and realizable, yet invisible and far away. The shift toward "pure money" may express the modern world's absorption in what Oswald Spengler called in his *Decline of the West* "abstraction," yet at the same time, it gives unforgettable *psychoanalytic* expression to money's magical character, its capacity to represent the *absent object,* to harbor within its illusory existence those transitional aims which derive from the infant's traumatic *separation* from the parent. What is emerging purely is the pure expression of the human *inner* world.

Goods and More Goods

Our analysis would be conspicuously incomplete were it to overlook *consumerism,* that aspect of the present order which directly engages the citizenry as a whole. What emerges here is plain enough: everything in the system, and that includes the state, is geared toward manipulating the "consumer" into a steady, uninterrupted urge to *buy products, to possess things.* Indeed, it is precisely this manipulation that stands at the center of the entire setup. To accomplish such an end, to "bring it off," the controllers of the marketplace must create the illusion that nothing is going on out there except the exercise of choice, that the individuals in the society, the *targets,* are entirely free to make their own decisions. "It is possible," writes Galbraith (1972, 217), "that people need to believe that they are unmanaged if they are to be managed effectively."

When we examine this "management" even briefly, we realize that it takes the form of an unflagging propaganda on behalf of goods. Again in the words of Galbraith (208),

from early morning until late at night, people are informed of the services rendered by goods—of their profound indispensibility. Every feature and facet of every product having been studied for selling points, these are then described with talent, gravity, and an aspect of profound concern as the source of health, happiness, social achievement, or improved community standing. Even minor qualities of unimportant commodities are enlarged upon with a solemnity which would not be unbecoming in an announcement of the combined return of Christ and all the apostles. More important services, such as the advantages of whiter laundry, are treated with proportionately greater gravity. The consequence is that while goods become ever more abundant they do not seem to be any less important. On the contrary, it requires an act of will to imagine that anything else is so important.

The point is, goods are what the industrial system supplies. Advertising, by making goods important, makes the industrial system important and thus sustains the social significance, the prestige, of the corporate structure. Because the well-being or "health" of the "economy" is totally dependent upon the public's continuous *expenditure* of money, it is vital not merely to get people to spend, it is dangerous to allow them to *save*. It is by *consuming products* that individuals serve the industrial order. The very system of taxation itself, and even the rate of inflation, are managed to ensure a steady rate of profit to the companies, and in this, of course, the *state* lends its support. In a very real sense, it *plans* the savings of its "citizens."

Most goods, needless to say, are not required in any genuine material sense; they have primarily a psychic appeal. They provide a sense of personal accomplishment, or equality with the neighbors; they "take one's mind off things," or enhance confidence in the sexual sphere. "The industrial system serves wants which are psychological in origin and hence admirably subject to management. Although a hungry man cannot be persuaded as between bread and a circus, a well-nourished man can. . . . The further a man is removed from physical needs the more he is open to persuasion—or management—as to what he buys. This is, perhaps, the most important consequence for the economics of increasing affluence" (Galbraith, 1972, 202). Surely one cannot miss the *transitional* significance in all of this. To go to the heart of the matter, capitalism, in its present form, *exploits the psychological equivalence of money and goods* in such a way as to lay the accent on goods, goods which *represent money*, which *are* money at the level of unconscious mentation. As Roheim observed, it is not merely "coin" as such that comes to signify the body of the object, either as a direct substitute (in primitive culture) or as a symbol of control (in the capitalist era). Wealth *in any form* can serve the magical purpose of dual-unity by becoming a surrogate for the maternal figure.

The ubiquitous "public images" which support the industrial system provide still another insight into the transitional indications of power and security, as psychological avenues to transitional fulfillment at the level of individual desire; goods are offered in such a way as to become loved and worshipped as symbols of the *national purpose.* In the prevailing ideology of the industrial state, what the corporation produces, what the consumer purchases, and what the nation is accomplishing are connected inextricably at the emotional level. Our current social organization, our current "democracy," Eli Sagan (1985, 375, 222) reminds us, "is the least dependent upon fundamental kinship ties of any political system ever invented, and as a result it generates an unusual share of anxiety, paranoia, and the need to express aggression outward, toward the world." Sagan also observes, "slowly and painfully, society has been attempting over thousands of years to construct new forms of attachment and reassurance that would compensate us for our kinship paradise lost." The link between the modern economic setup and what this paragraph describes as the "national purpose" is solidified by these statements. Our passionate chase after *goods* ("good objects") is, first, our attempt to discover "new forms of attachment" in our alienated, kin-less culture, our paradise *lost.* We shop, we buy, we *consume,* we feed ourselves "products," in a pathetic, obsessive struggle to deny the absence of those flesh-and-blood contacts that formerly tied people together and provided them with precious compensation for the *loss* of the object which characterized the separation phase of infancy. Second, we make our obsessive economic activity, our endless oral frenzy, a part of the "national purpose," or indeed the national purpose *itself* ("the richest country in the world!"), in an effort to convince ourselves that we *do* in fact live in a genuine society, in a truly cohesive group, in a shared community of emotion and intention. We know deep down, however, that loneliness and isolation are the rule.

Richard Koenigsberg (1977, 39) writes in his book, *The Psychoanalysis of Racism, Revolution, and Nationalism,* "where once the individual's connection to the community had been defined in terms of relationships with persons *present* in the immediate physical environment, now this connection is defined in terms of relationships with persons *not present* in the immediate physical environment." Koenigsberg goes on, "there are a number of important changes which are associated with this shift in the nature of community. One of the most important of these . . . is that a national community may be more easily 'turned off' than a physically present community. If one does not wish to 'interact' with one's 'friends' from the mass-media, one may turn off the television, stop reading newspapers, etc." What this brings home vividly is the following: It is not merely *goods* that serve a transitional purpose in our current, "loose," democratic society; the media in the widest sense, television, newspapers, magazines, films, *all* the "nonpresent" forms of attachment, serve such a purpose as they foster the so-called global village. We do not turn to these entities and then away from them again in pure, conscious *choice*. We turn to and away in *compulsion*, in *ambivalence*, in *confusion*, and even in *sorrow*. We turn to and away because these "nonpresent" forms mirror or reflect the nature of our ordinary awareness in a deep psychological way. The psyche may grow toward individuation, and this may destroy the old kinship bonds and the direct, supportive style of social interaction. But the psyche does not relinquish its transitional aim, its life and death struggle to hold on to the object and its concomitant tendency to *project* that struggle into its environmental creations. We are dealing here with a *whole perceptual orientation* that is ultimately *symptomatic* in nature.

The Body of the State: Motherlands, Fatherlands, Homelands, and the People

Among the most compelling environmental creations into which the psyche projects the separation/union conflict is the nation, the state, the communal body and the ideological framework within which it invariably exists. This was very strongly indicated in the previous section, of course, where we noted the way in which economic aims can get bound up with the national purpose. When Murray Edelman (1988) observes in his book *Constructing the Political Spectacle* that a nation characteristically has at the metaphorical level its birth ("The Birth of a Nation"), its parents ("The Founding Fathers"), its "life history" (including its "youth" and "maturity"), its "enemies" and its "friends," and that it is routinely regarded from within by its citizens as a kind of "family," he only reminds us of the degree to which a nation can exist in an individual's mind as a *psychological object* in the full, psychodynamic sense—something that is also disclosed by common expressions such as motherland, homeland, fatherland, sacred soil, home turf, Mother Russia, body politic, and so on. During the course of the past few decades

psychoanalysis has become increasingly aware of the psychody-
namic dimension of nations, groups, and leaders through such
works as Freud's *Group Psychology and the Analysis of the Ego,*
Wilhelm Reich's *Mass Psychology of Fascism,* Ernest Becker's
Escape From Evil, and most recently Richard Koenigsberg's
Symbiosis and Separation.

Exploring the "revolutionary behavior patterns" of Hitler and
Lenin, Koenigsberg (1989, 39) maintains they are best regarded
as "counterphobic defense against the regressive fantasy of
merger." Hitler is "deeply attached to 'Germany,' Lenin to 'the
people'—these are the symbolic equivalents of the symbiotic
mother." Hitler wishes to be "one" with Germany; Lenin wishes
to be "one" with the people. Each of them "idealizes the object
of his love and believes that any action undertaken is justifiable
if done in the name of this love-object." In each case, however,
"it would appear that the *other side* of the idealized wish for
union with the object is a *passive dependency*," the psychic
consequence "of the infantile, symbiotic attachment to the
mother." This "passive-dependent wish," Koenigsberg continues,
"is *projected* onto other objects in social reality, various 'classes'
of persons, and the effort is made to 'kill' one's dependency by
killing the object which symbolizes the dependency. The object
which is killed is the infantile, symbiotic ego as it attaches to
the omnipotent mother." Revolutionaries such as Hitler and Lenin "are trying to 'kill off' that part of themselves which symbolizes their dependent, symbiotic attachment, but they have
undertaken an impossible task because the wish to preserve the
symbiotic bond in the form of an attachment to the nation or
the people is precisely what fuels the revolutionary struggle."
The revolutionary, then, is one who "simultaneously refuses to
relinquish symbiosis and who struggles against the burden of
symbiosis." He is "stuck in the middle" and his revolutionary
struggle is "permanent."

Extending such insights to the cultural sphere as a whole
Koenigsberg (57) asserts that "what ties the human being to the
institutions of society is precisely the projection of the infantile
situation." The human connection to the social world "is fueled
by the attachment to inner objects; the institutions of society
attain their power and hold upon individuals because they serve
as containers for infantile energies and emotions. The objects of
culture become symbols of inner objects, and because they do
we idealize and become attached to these objects." In this way,
the "symbiotic fantasy of connection is not abandoned but trans-

ferred onto new objects, which serve to replicate the infantile experience of connectedness." The human being "attaches himself to the omnipotent culture just as he was once attached to the omnipotent mother," and the "world is experienced not as an external reality but as a transitional object." When one "speaks of the 'duality' of self and world, one is not necessarily speaking of a separate self or subject who perceives a separate world 'out there' as an external reality." Rather, "the world as an object of perception is conceived as a symbol of the symbiotic half of the self; ultimately, as an extension of one's own body."

This culture itself, civilization itself, must be viewed in the context of the separation/union struggle and the projective "spells" that it engenders. As we noted in Chapter 2, following Roheim's (1971, 131) famous remarks, civilization originates "in delayed infancy and its function is security." It is "a huge network of more or less successful attempts to protect mankind from the danger of object-loss, the colossal efforts made by a baby who is afraid of being left alone in the dark." Howard Stein puts the matter somewhat differently when he writes in a series of recent and remarkable articles that "the experience of group fantasy is the *narcissism of the no-difference* among those who together identify themselves as identical." The "first person singular" is experienced as the "first person plural: I am we." The "mere fact of joining a group (from culture to party) elicits the fantasy of being affiliated kin." Such feelings, observes Stein, "derive not exclusively from one's family of origin but from the very earliest relationship with the mother. . . . Group fantasy is not 'like' a dissociated trance-state, it *is* a trance in origin, structure, and function." If "most human behavior is ritual," then the "reality to which most culture and history is responsive is that of inner anxiety" (Stein 1981, 246). And in what is perhaps an even more striking presentation of the issue, Stein (1984, 304) maintains that "dependency, neoteny, helplessness, separation, loss, and death are the problems for which men design cultures—not only religions—as solutions. Sadly, through culture thus far, men have only succeeded in relocating the problem rather than in solving it by working it through. Cultural symbolism and ritualization only forever postpone the solution." Indeed, they "incapacitate men by serving as cozening bromides that narcotize them away from reality."

The point is, there can be just as much magical thinking, just as much acting-out, just as much fusion and unconscious omnipotence brought to our attachment to nation, party, leader, or group of whatever kind as there is brought to our attachment to gold or to Goddess. More particularly, the attachments to nation, ideology, and leader are rooted in the very same transitional dynamics, the very same psychological longings and anxieties, that stand behind the "bromide" of modern Witchcraft. The behaviors that many of us evince in the economic and political spheres, or in our devotion to the "fruits of success," are in a very real psychoanalytical sense a kind of secular Wicca with versions of the Goddess at their center and with varieties of bewitchment as their goal.

To recover from this, to pass beyond it or at least to begin to do so, is, as Stein implies, to *see* it all fully and clearly in the brightest, plainest psychological light, to *look* at it, to trace its roots to the primal anxieties that gave rise to the bewitchment— in short, as Stein declares, to work it through. Only this will allow us to awaken from the trance; only this will allow us to attain that emotional place where we know we can exist satisfactorily without embedding ourselves in the group body or identifying ourselves powerfully with the leader; only this will allow us to realize that our survival does not depend on possessions and colossal profits, that we can exist with less, that we can make it on our own, forging reasonable, thoughtful, limited ties to cultural institutions, including banks and stock exchanges. *Unless* we do this, unless we disrupt the narcosis, we keep very much alive the potential for all the madness, greed, rapine, bigotry, fanaticism, superstition, and plain stupidity that have plagued the human species for several thousand years. Unless we do this, unless we "evolve" past the bewitchment, we merely stumble ahead as dangerously as ever. Indeed, the Witches' laudable goals of ecological responsibility and economic and social justice will come about more smoothly and more swiftly as we begin to appreciate the degree to which our ties to nation, party, profit, and cult *are all similarly grounded* in the unconscious tie to the object and in the emotional crises of separation and loss that attend the early period.

The Truth as a Psychological Object: Scientific Endeavors

For centuries, in the tradition of Descartes and his followers, science was *rigorous*, that is, scientists believed in an objective truth, in an objective reality, and they were convinced that the strict application of empirical-inductive methodologies to the world around them would expose that reality, that truth, to their inquiring eyes. A perfect illustration derives from the life and work of André-Marie Ampère, "the first investigator to quantify the magnetic effects of electric current, and a pioneer in the philosophy of science" (Williams 1989, 90). After 1827, toward the close of his career, Ampère's health began to decline. He abandoned scientific research and returned to his theoretical writings. Here he rediscovered "some of the inspiration of his early youth" (ibid., 97). He was "enraptured by Leibniz' doctrine of preestablished harmony," which held that "man's mind is a copy, albeit an imperfect one, of the mind of God." Since man's reasoning process is an image of God's, "the human mind should be able to understand the universe through a process of pure reason." There should be a "preexisting harmony between the laws of the universe and the reasoning powers of mankind." Thus, argued Ampère, "if one could outline all the sciences the human mind could possibly construct," one would have the "basic key to all possible truth," since the "mind is structured in a way that corresponds directly to the structure of the universe: all knowledge is but the reflection of the unity of the divine mind" (ibid.). We now know better, or at least the vast majority of us claim that we do.

We know that science can only give us a rigorous presentation of "the truth" as it appears to the human point of view; we know that "the facts," whatever they may be, are loaded perforce with assumptions and preconceptions which are rooted inextricably in our biological and psychological make-up. As good post-Kantians, we know that we will never have a God's-eye look at the universe, that we will never behold the "thing-in-itself." In the words of Jeremy Campbell (1982, 111), "no final, wrapped-up, all-inclusive view of reality will ever be perfected. The nature of language, the forms of logic, the duality of matter beneath the surface we observe, the power of rules to generate new structures, the limits to knowledge, the special character of complex as opposed to simple systems, all point to this conclusion. In this respect, science and art, philosophy and politics, history and psychology meet on common ground." The "exact sciences," concludes Campbell, have been "disturbed to their very foundations." But what is more than this, we now recognize that the very *belief* in objective truth, objective reality, perfect certainty, and complete knowledge of the world through scientific endeavor *is itself* an expression of the separation/union conflict, *is itself* an instance of the wish for omnipotence and fusion that is tied historically to the symbiotic object.

There *is* an objective reality, says this wish; there *is* a universal truth, and to *know* it is to *have* it, to *grasp* it and *cleave* to it. No longer is there a mysterious universe "out there" from which we are cut off; rather, there is a coherent, ordered entity that has *revealed* itself to us (as a good object should do); it is *familiar* (as in "family"); it has been *penetrated;* it is ours in perfect knowledge, made accessible to us by our great instrument of science. We have omniscience, which is a variety of omnipotence, and we have fusion with "the truth." The quest for certainty, in John Dewey's expression, is over, as well as the Cartesian doubt. Beholding the mind of God, or something pretty close to it, we feel secure, and *limitless.*

What I am trying to underscore is that the whole matter of "the truth" in recent times is not merely a philosophical or epistemological issue; it is an *emotional issue with an unconscious aspect.* The "uncertainty principle" of Heisenberg sparked furious debate among both geniuses and the educated population generally because it triggered, along with intellectual puzzles, feelings of insecurity, helplessness, lostness, and impotency. It made everyone confront a dice-playing God who could not be trusted in the way Ampère's God could be trusted. (This was the kind of God Descartes feared and argued against in his *Meditations.*) The "uncertainty principle" forced us to give up a profoundly treasured ideal and a substitute for religion, a "love-object" that scientists are *still* reluctant to relinquish in their hearts.

"When pressed on the matter," writes the physicist Roger S. Jones (1982, 206), "most scientists will concede that all physical theories are tentative and approximate and that there is no clear conception of physical reality in modern quantum theory." However, continues Jones, "such disclaimers are made in the interest of fair play, so to speak. They do not characterize the way scientists behave and think in their everyday activities of research and teaching nor in their conversations with each other." There, the "fundamental idolatry" that "an external physical world exists as an objective reality independent of the human mind" and that the "business of science" is the "discovery and description" of this world reigns as vigorously as ever. The scientists, in Jones's words (208), "cannot be parted" from their old, idolatrous notion.

Nietzsche (1966, 2) asked teasingly, at the height of the nineteenth century's pursuit of the truth, "Supposing truth is a woman, what then?" We cannot know *exactly* what Nietzsche meant by this, but today through psychoanalysis we can see a profound, striking connection to our contextual points; that is, if the search for "the truth" or the quest for certainty as exemplified preeminently by science is in some significant measure a search for dual-unity, for lost omnipotence and merger, and if this search is tied inextricably to the original object of life's first years, the object who enforces separation, enforces differentiation, enforces the end of symbiosis, then truth *does* turn out in a way Nietzsche brilliantly intuited, to be a woman, the woman we *won't give up.* Nietzsche (1967, 18) asked in another place, "Is the resolve to be so scientific about everything perhaps a kind of fear of, an escape from, pessimism? . . . a sort of cowardice and falseness, . . . a ruse?" For "pessimism" I would substitute the narcissistic wound that derives from the loss of fusion and omnipotence, and for "ruse" I would substitute unconscious defense.

Beauty Is Truth, Truth Beauty

The "aim of science," writes Louis Berger (1985, 101), is "to try to construct a coherent and intellectually satisfying picture of the world." Henry J. Steffens (1974, 96) expresses it this way: "Science is a search for the hidden unity behind the confusing multiplicity of events." Scientific theories do not emerge automatically or even rigorously from "data" or "the facts"; they are "creations of the human mind, with its freely invented ideas and concepts" (ibid., 97), and as a recent issues of *The Sciences* makes clear, they are triggered in significant measure by the scientist's perception of beauty or symmetry in the details of the approach he is following. "Heisenberg did not depend on experimental evidence to validate his theory," writes Hans Christian von Baeyer (1990, 2), "that would come later. What convinced him that he was on the right track were the elegance, coherence, and inner beauty of his approach—in other words, its aesthetic qualities." Or again, this time in Dirac's words, "the research worker in his efforts to express the fundamental laws of nature in mathematical form should strive mainly for mathematical beauty" (ibid., 3). None of this, remarks von Baeyer (ibid.), "sounds a death knell for experiment. Wherever experimental evidence can be coaxed out of nature, it suffices to corroborate or refute a theory and serves as the sole arbiter of validity." But where evidence is "sparse or absent—as it is for a growing number of questions in physics—other criteria, including aesthetic ones, come into play in an essential way, both for formulating a theory and for evaluating it." Accordingly, it is "imperative that physicists know what they mean when they make appeals to such standards as elegance, coherence, and inner beauty." And the *nature* of "inner beauty," we then learn, resides in a detection of "likeness" between items that appear at first glance to be dissimilar, in other words, in a kind of *metaphorical perception,* such as "Einstein's theory that the ratio of the energies of two particles of light is equal to the ratio of their frequencies: Einstein's postulated relation between energy and frequency was completely unwarranted from the viewpoint of classical nineteenth-century physics" (ibid., 4). Thus science, like art, offers us not a photocopy of nature but a *recreation* of nature along specific, formal lines.

A theory, like a poem, is a certain kind of *projection,* and we find ourselves *compelled* by it because we *identify* with it at the formal, aesthetic level. The rules of science are there to govern or to control the creative, intuitive picture, to test it empirically, but the overall conceptualization, or "paradigm," is left wide open to the scientist's vision and sense of form. There can be no rules for intuition, yet in the background is form, the quest for order and coherence—an offspring of the same impulse that lies behind the aesthetic realm. Copernicus called the Ptolemaic system "monstrous" and worked to develop a scheme that would be more aesthetically pleasing. Today we make formal war on "chaos" itself with our "chaotic theories" and "fractal geometries." We want to systematize even systems that appear to be functions of infinitely unpredictable chaotic events. Nature *will* be ordered, *will* be coherent, *will* be mastered, we implicitly insist, down to its last quark or cloud or coastline. Now, when we remind ourselves once again that one of the "essential functions of the mother-infant unity" is the "provision of order, harmony, and organization," and that the symbiotic mother "by empathetically and reliably attuning herself to her infant's signals conveys an ordering rhythmicity," and when we remind ourselves further that the "optimal state which the developing child seeks to maintain or restore is one of order and coherence," the state he knew and relished during the time of symbiosis (Behrends and Blatt, 1985, 18), we appreciate the extent to which formal scientific endeavors may engage the separation/

union conflict, the longing for coherence and order which is a facet not only of aesthetic pursuits but of the primal, dual-unity relation. In Nietzsche's provocative terms, it may not only be truth that is a woman; a theory may be a woman, too.

This does not mean, of course, that science is ultimately meaningless, or illusory, or regressive, or a "ruse." It means only that the scientists who do it are just as capable of bewitchment as the Witches are, and that their bewitchment (when it occurs) derives from the very same infantile place from which the trances of usury or ideology or nationalism or Wicca derive. To spell this out in a spirit of shared humanity (and theoretical inquiry!), is simply to give the scientist a chance to know himself better than he perhaps presently does, and more particularly, to understand the ease with which his scientific endeavors get mixed up with his own dreams of omnipotence and fusion, and with the aims of power-hungry, money-hungry governments and corporations. To put it somewhat differently, as scientists come to appreciate fully the degree to which their endeavors can reactivate the aims and wishes of the early period, they will find themselves better prepared to cut their way through the jungles of their own narcissism and dependency, as well as through the mystifications held out to them by cultural bodies eager for profit and power. They will find themselves more capable of getting the *psychological object* out of their *objectivity*, of fulfilling the aims of their science as opposed to the aims of their magical, unconscious agendas. "I reject the myth of reality as external to the human mind," writes the physicist Roger S. Jones in the Preface to his book, *Physics as Metaphor* (1982, ix); "and I acknowledge consciousness as the source of the cosmos. It is mind that we see reflected in matter. Physical science is a metaphor with which the scientist, like the poet, creates and extends meaning and value in the quest for understanding and purpose." To add our understanding of the separation/union conflict to this magnificent credo, to see "mind as reflected in matter" as mind with separation and power on its mind, is to go a step further in the way of deepening and humanizing our study of the world.

Computer! Oh, Computer!

The psychological and perceptual issues we have been exploring swirl revealingly around the most recent of our great scientific inventions, the computer. It offers itself to its manipulator as a powerful little world, a powerful little universe, a kind of microcosm that can be totally mastered, totally controlled, in such a way as to offset at the unconscious level the traumatic loss of omnipotence experienced during the separation phase. When the researcher puts his information, his models, his intellectual creations, into his "switched on" computing machine, writes Harry Kleinberg (a computer expert), he "suddenly finds himself in possession of a mythical world whose fate he totally controls" (Kleinberg 1977, 176). One does not have to reflect very long or very hard to appreciate the potential for bewitchment in such a situation.

Again and again in both scientific and popular current literature one discovers passages that reveal the extent to which the computer has become in our minds a magical, quasi-human object promising the omnipotence and immortality traditionally offered the worshipper by religious cults, including the cult of Wicca. The fantasies take two characteristic forms, one of which has already been captured for us by Kleinberg. *We* are the masters of the awesome machine; we control it, and by extension, we can control others *through* it. A recent issue of *Time* offers a cover story whose author marvels over the "raw power," the "blazing speed" of the new "supercomputers," and, in a revealing metaphor, goes on to discuss the current technologists who are in the process of learning to master these "dumb brutes" (Elmer-DeWitt 1988, 40). We might call this the master-slave fantasy: We become omnipotent through our control of the incredible mechanical object, the "brute."

Conversely, we have the fantasy of the computer as the quasi-human, magical object of *worship. It* becomes the god, the idol, the source of immortality and power; we become, simply, the means of *attaining* it. Barrow and Tipler (1986, 615), writing in *The Anthropic Cosmological Principle* and confronting the ineluctable doom of our species as the universe approaches its "Final State," maintain that our "civilization" and our "values" need not perish, ever. "From the behavioral point of view intelligent *machines* may be regarded as people," they say, and they go on in a disturbingly confused, schizoid passage, "these machines may be our ultimate heirs, our ultimate descendants, because ... they could survive forever the extreme conditions of the Final State. Our civilization may be continued indefinitely by them, and the values of humankind may thus be transmitted to ... distant futurity." Robert Jastrow (1978, 47), in another *Time* article called "Toward an Intelligence Beyond Man's," also sees the computer taking on an existence of its own, reproducing itself, superseding the people who originally fashioned it, creating its own culture and civilization out of silicon, and becoming, in Jastrow's words, "the master race" of the future, a "species" far beyond anything paltry humans might achieve. Similar sentiments come recently from a group called the Artificial Lifers (or A Lifers) whose perspective is described in an article by Michael Schrage (1990, D19). They regard humans "as mere evolutionary stepping stones on the path to a more highly evolved, highly intelligent silicon-based species," a "race" of "complex and powerful creatures" with a "sophistication" far beyond anything we can presently imagine. Our chief distinction as a form of life will reside in our being "the first species" (that we know of) "to create its own successors." All this we might call the computer as savior fantasy. The machine becomes the omnipotent, immortal object and, at the unconscious level, we projectively blend into it and live forever through it.

Preoccupations with power and immortality are not, however, the only ones that attach themselves to this mechanical device; *transitional* preoccupations, the dependent longing for proximity and fusion, the dread of separation, rejection, and loss also find their way to the world of the computer. A recent issue of *Omni,* for example, holds that newly developed computers are becoming "curious, sensitive, and quick to comprehend"; soon they will "possess the vision and virtue of a six-year-old" (Fjermedal 1988, 45). Has there ever been a greater insult to childhood? One model, according to this author, is almost ready to serve its possessor as a "moral advisor" (ibid., 50), helping him to "make decisions and solve dilemmas that crop up in everyday life." Ultimately, such a machine is designed to become not only a "personal companion" and "best friend" but an antidote to loneliness and even an "alternative to marriage" (ibid., 78). One Arthur Harkins, a cultural anthropologist at the University of Minnesota, writes on this score: "We could build machines that make perpetually available to us the characteristics of lovemaking, intelligence, and sociability. Even if we made them as appliances, not as fully intelligent devices, they could still have a lot of these traits, including bubbling conversations" (ibid.). The best thing about such "machines," reports *Omni,* is that they never "fail" (ibid., 79). We might call this "the computer as good shepherd fantasy": The transitional object returns, not as a goddess but as a lump of intricately wired plastic in our pockets—an idol befitting a technological and narcissistic age.

These projections and fantasies become more psychoanalytically intelligible as we link them to additional metaphors commonly employed in the computational realm. Like the maternal object herself, the computer is integrally associated with problems of feeding. Information derived from the perceptual life is fed into it, and it, in turn, feeds back information symbiotically. It may be said, in fact, that all questions bound up with the control of the computer and its control of us are directly related to metaphors of feeding and feedback. One of the first lessons psychoanalysis taught us was that of the unconscious meaning of words. We must not forget that lesson here. Again, the computer, like the maternal object of the early time, cannot be manipulated without careful consideration of its positive and negative poles, its tendency to operate through simple oppositions inherent in terms such as "and," "not," "or"—in a word, its *split,* binary nature. If one feeds the machine appropriately along the positive and/or negative channels, it "accepts" what one offers; if one feeds the machine wrongly, it "rejects" one's offering and will not "come 'round" until the feeder has determined the correct "input," the input that will be incorporated into the "guts" of the creature so that it may work its transformative processes upon it, eventually feeding back the desired response. The unconscious significance of such material is completed, of course, as we recall the current, widespread tendency to present the computer in *art, literature,* and *film* as a quasi-human entity, an *object* in the psychological sense of the term. As is often the case, the creative, imaginative expressions of the species—a species whose emotional life is determined by the manner in which it processes the *information* of the early years—harbor its deep, unrecognized wishes and fears.

As for the question, is there evidence that human beings *do* respond to the computer as an object, evidence that comes not from indirect sources such as *Time, Omni,* and the movie *Star Wars* but from controlled, systematic investigation, the answer is, to be sure. Exploring meticulously the responses of eighty-eight graduate students who were asked to write narratives based upon their use of the computer, John Broughton (1988, 3) discovered what he called "the discourse of desire" lurking beneath the disguise of "electronic rationality."[5] Generally "reified" by subjects as an "alien mechanism" (10), the computer fostered various levels of anxiety and was typically associated with "closed and constricted space" and with the regrettable "thingification" of the world. Many experienced a hypnotic and

ambivalent attraction to the machine, and felt they were somehow escaping into its manipulative potential. Broughton speaks
of alternating fantasies of "fission" and "fusion" among his subjects, terms that strikingly recall the separation/union conflict
exemplified in Mahler and others.

In several instances narratives disclosed responses closely associated with feeding and food, with what Broughton terms
"orality"; for example, "Joy sat down at the computer. She wished
she had sometime to eat"; "he rose from his seat . . . and grabbed
a bag of Doritos." Broughton writes, "there appears to be some
implicit parallel between the computer and the oven, drawing
closer to the symbolic juxtaposition of the system of information
flow and the system of nutrient flow" (ibid., 14). Also present
persistently among responses were issues of domination, mastery, and control, and accompanying fantasies of an aggressive
and/or sexual nature: "The light suddenly came on and she
physically recoiled. But she was more powerful than the machine. Well, at least she felt she was more powerful. She started
wondering whether in fact the computer was more powerful
than she" (12). Broughton observes toward the conclusion of his
study that his findings "parallel closely the clinical and empirical
findings on the disruptions occurring in expressive relations
between infants and their mothers. . . . The operator is positioned in relation to the technological device in a way that
evokes the original experience of heteronomy, one that fuses a
need for care with a desire for the other's power" (22).[6]

The point is, the kind of emotion (or affect) that underlies the
"higher" fantasies of the computer as companion, alien thing,
immortal god, lover, and brute derives in considerable measure
from the early period, from the world of the infant and the
mother, particularly as that world precipitates the timeless human preoccupation with omnipotence, fusion, separation, and
mortality. The computer is merely the latest item to be dragged
into this old arena and made to bear the obsessional weight
traditionally placed upon pharaohs, kings, totem animals, standing stones, and golden calves. A recent documentary film (Japan-
American series 1989) on Japanese business practices developed
by Telejapan and narrated by Dick Cavett shows Japanese work-
ers parading around their factory in full religious garb and
shouting over and over again to the beat of ancient drums,
"Computer! Computer! Univac! Hooray! Hooray!" Here, our psy-
choanalyses of economics, religion, science, and technology
come together in a single moment.

Strong AI

It is not simply the machine, however, that stands at the center today: The issue of programming is just as conspicuous. Indeed, the question of artificial intelligence, or Strong AI as it is called, the issue of whether or not we can produce a program that duplicates human thought processes, is one of the liveliest topics around. And it captures for us unforgettably the extent to which the old obsessions of omnipotence and fusion continue to bewitch the species.

The central argument against the feasibility of Strong AI may be found in Hubert Dreyfus's volume, *What Computers Can't Do* (1972). Because human thought is characteristically *contextual* (as opposed to atomistic or discrete), and because its human context is infinitely unpredictable in respect of its potential for associational details, there is no way for a manufactured program to duplicate it truly. To think in human terms is to bring to the process thousands, even millions of mentational and affective nuances (both conscious and unconscious) that render it plainly and simply unprogrammable. Accordingly, individuals involved in Strong AI are ultimately involved in a kind of schizoid wild-goose chase. They cannot or will not perceive the rich emotional and biological context in which human thinking transpires. If they could, they would see the sheer silliness in a remark such as R. Colin Johnson's (1990, 28) that soon "our electronic offspring" will "become alive in the truest sense." To produce a computer that is "alive in the truest sense" would be a thousand times more difficult than to preprogram the exact trajectory of each and every air particle flying around in a violent year-long windstorm.

The most recent and influential voice of dissent in the area of Strong AI is that of John Searle (1990) whose central argument is a variation upon Dreyfus's. What Searle maintains, essentially, is that *simulation* is not *duplication.* Even if one were to produce a program that simulated human thinking, it would not *be* human thinking because it would not possess understanding. In support of this, Searle offers what has now becomes the notorious "Chinese room" in which an individual who has learned to manipulate Chinese characters responds correctly to questions passed to him through a slit. Although it appears that this individual understands Chinese, he, in fact, understands nothing because, as Searle expresses it, "syntax is not semantics" (ibid., 30). So it is with Strong AI. It will not produce human thought,

which is biological, organic, and linked to contextual understanding, any more than a program designed to simulate diges-
tion will actually digest any food. The problem, says Searle, is
that proponents of Strong AI erroneously take human thought
to be something that occurs apart from, or independent of, the
human body; they see it as a kind of pure, mentalistic phenomenon, which it is not. Human thinking and mechanical, computational operations simply have nothing to do with one another.
They occur in separate, unrelated spheres. One can run as many
simulations of sexual fantasy as one wishes, but in the end one
will not get his computer to pant.

The positions of Dreyfus and Searle have been challenged over
the years by a variety of computer experts including, most recently and most notably, Paul and Patricia Churchland (1990,
32), who argue that "systems which mimic the brain" might well
lead to what they designate as "conscious machines." Explicitly
attacking both Dreyfus's contentions and Searle's "Chinese
room," the Churchlands declare: "Of course, at present no one
knows the function that would produce the output behavior of
a conscious person . . . but the Church and Turing results assure
us that a suitable SM machine could compute it" (32). They
continue, "even though Searle's Chinese room may appear to be
'semantically dark' he is in no position to insist on the strength
of this appearance, that rule-governed symbol manipulation can
never constitute semantic phenomena, especially when people
have only an uninformed commonsense understanding of the
semantic and cognitive phenomena that need to be explained"
(ibid., 35). And then, in what we may regard as their chief utterance, one that impinges upon not only this discussion but the
whole position of Strong AI, they write: "If one can just set in
motion an appropriately structured internal dance of syntactic
elements, appropriately connected to inputs and outputs, it can
produce the same cognitive states and achievements found in
human beings." The problem, of course, is that where human
beings are concerned there *is* no such thing as "cognitive state"
in the sense the Churchlands mean.

Always and forever human thought is tied to the physical organism, to the conscious, preconscious, and unconscious realms
and their infinitely varied affective and instinctual expressions
which, when taken together, constitute the interdependent system that happens to be *us*. The "system" of "mimicry" to which
the Churchlands refer (32) has nothing whatever to do *ulti-*

mately with the system of thought in which our mind-brains consist. In a very real sense, the Churchlands' reliance on *systems theory* hoists them with their own petard. It is precisely the *full human system of thought with its infinite affective and unconscious associations rooted in both body and mind simultaneously* that renders *their* system inadequate. When Freud discovered parapraxes or slips of the tongue, the significance of which we may now more fully appreciate, he revealed once and for all that our *whole* mind, both conscious and unconscious, is at work as we process information. *This* is what computer programmers must "mimic" if they are going to yield machines that harbor *human* consciousness. Heaven help them, for it is only in a mechanical world of mechanical thought, a world with no human beings in it, that machines may be made to "think" in some realistic sense.

As to why the practitioners of Strong AI persist in their attempts to produce a "conscious machine," there are, of course, a number of explanations, including the mechanical fascination of the business and the money provided by gullible bureaucrats. But among the explanations is the following: The practitioners persist because the dream of omnipotence and fusion persists; they persist because the dualistic belief in an "objective reality" (Churchland 1990, 37) which we can penetrate and with which we can merge persists; they persist because, like many other people, they have succeeded in denying the ineluctable presence of the body and the emotions in certain human pursuits; they persist because they have managed to remain in the empyrean of science where they contemplate abstractly, in a "logical space" as Wittgenstein might put it, the so-called "cognitive states" of their fellow, fleshly mortals. In short, the dream of a program for consciousness and the machine that it will bring to life is the latest dream of the separation/union conflict. The symbiotic mother returns yet again to inspire our narcissistic grandiosity: We will reproduce ourselves mechanically. We will make ourselves all-knowing and immortal. We don't *need* our flesh-and-blood mothers anymore. We can separate from them forever. *We* are omnipotent now, or, as the Witches would say, *we* are the Goddess. Although the practitioners of Strong AI may cringe at the idea, there is just as much magical thinking and denial, just as much bewilderment, in their Faustian attempts to produce a conscious computer as there is in the Witches' attempt to draw down the moon.

A Concluding Word

The separation/union conflict, with its related narcissistic issues, in an integral aspect of our development at all ages. In a very real psychological sense, the separation/union conflict *is* our human nature. As we struggle with it, or more specifically as we struggle to heal the wounds of lost omnipotence, lost fusion, lost bliss, we are constantly tempted to choose the regressive pathways toward which we are guided by the symbols of religion, economics, ideology, science, and many other cultural spheres. We have only to join this party or movement or cult, say our narcissistic hopes, we have only to get rich, or invent this extraordinary device, or become involved in scientific questing after "the truth," to find a shortcut to the emotional perfection we are seeking. In some instances, of course, the chosen route is blatantly pathological and delusional, divorced from ordinary reality, absorbed in a private world of inner objects, and neglectful of the social realm and the humans who in large measure comprise it. The bewitchments we have been exploring here, including the Craft, are not of this nature, generally speaking. With the exceptions of astral travel, auric healing, and channeling which border on the delusional and pathological (just as a fanatical commitment to Nazism or behaviorism might so border) the conduct at which we have been looking falls more or less into the normal range. And that is what is so disturbing. Many of our most normative, everyday, taken-for-granted behaviors and activities are obviously *loaded* with regressive, narcissistic longings for omnipotence and fusion, for the magical, narcotic solution to the dilemmas of life.

At the same time, to complicate the business further, the separation/union conflict, and the narcissistic quest to which it gives rise, is the source of much that is good and great in human affairs. Here is the motive for independence, adventure, imagination, heroism, social and intellectual accomplishment, including economic success and shared prosperity. We relinquish the original object; we find appropriate and healthful substitutes that become egotic goals in their own right, free of early, compulsive associations, and embodying our highest standards of mental and physical excellence. All this is fueled in significant measure by our need to *get separate,* to carve out a universe of our own, and to actualize the love and enthusiasm we internalized early on in a differentiated, personal way. I do not believe the two sides of the separation/union conflict make the search for human improvement hopeless or futile, although they may make it very, very difficult. To wake from our waking dream, to perceive the extent to which our normal, everyday conduct is fraught with the aims and purposes of the wounded, secret self, is to relinquish certain illusions, certain precious defenses and triumphs, and that can be painful. But what we gain through the process may make it worth the anxiety and discomfort: clearer vision and a more honest relation to the world and all its creatures. The Witches, in their obsession with omnipotence and magic, in their concomitant desire to depend on the parental surrogate, to be passive and secure upon the bosom of the *magna mater,* and in their passionate concern with social justice and ecological responsibility help us not only to see the separation/union conflict in splendid, unforgettable detail but also to distinguish more sharply than we perhaps have distinguished hitherto the progressive from the regressive in human behavior.

Notes

Chapter 2. Merger, Separation, and Omnipotence

1. Daniel Stern, in his recent and influential book, *The Interpersonal World of the Infant* (New York: Basic Books, 1985), takes issue with Mahler's postulation of an autistic phase. For Stern, the infant is forging his sense of self from the moment of birth onward. Stern does acknowledge Mahler's symbiotic stage; however, he calls it "the psychologically nourishing selfobject milieu" (108), following Wolf, in an effort to keep the emphasis on the infant's separate psychological self. Stern's modifications of Mahler have attracted a good deal of attention and are worth exploring. Ultimately, in my view at least, they leave Mahler's overall scheme intact.

Chapter 3. A Psychoanalysis of Witchcraft Today

1. I am aware that Wiccan texts occasionally make a distinction between the Goddess and the particular items in her domain. Simos (1979, 25), for example, writes that "all things are one, yet each thing is separate, individual, unique"—a view that is echoed by Farrar (1987, 3). Such distinctions, however, mean little in the Wiccan sea of metaphors and symbols announcing the divine, salvational fusion, the termination of the old, dreaded separation. Indeed, such distinctions emerge ultimately as afterthoughts or qualifications engendered by the anxiety that must at one level attend the powerful impulse toward merger with, or engulfment into, the Great Mother's body. They are the exceptions that prove the rule.

2. During the course of the Dini Petti talk show televised in Toronto on 13 October 1989, Tamarra James, High Priestess of the Wiccan Church of Canada (Toronto), told her fascinated audience, "You are the Goddess, you are divine, you are perfection, if only you would realize it." High Priestess James also made it clear that initiation into the Wiccan community was an excellent way to bring this realization about.

3. For a relatively recent psychoanalytic study of Witchcraft in West Africa, the reader might want to consult Henri Collomb's (1978) paper, "Witchcraft-Anthropophagia and Dyadic Relationship," published in *Psyche* 33: 463–82. Collomb's discussion highlights and deepens the picture of Witchcraft presented in Chapter 1 through the work of Kluckhohn and Roheim. For a summary of recent anthropological and psychological studies of Witchcraft and sorcery worldwide, the reader might want to consult Jeffrey B. Russell's *History of Witchcraft* (1980).

4. Witchcraft's use of James E. Lovelock's Gaia Hypothesis is worth noting here. According to Tim Beardsley (1989, 35), associate editor of the *Scientific American,* the hypothesis asserts that "all the animals and plants can be re-

garded as a single vast organism capable of manipulating the atmosphere, geosphere, and hydrosphere to suit its needs." What Beardsley calls "Lovelock's musings" were challenged by the scientific community upon their first appearance in the late 1960s, and they have now been thoroughly discredited and abandoned by all except "the scientifically innocent" (35). Wiccan texts routinely resort to Lovelock's hypothesis in an effort to prove that the Great Goddess is alive and well, and dwelling in our corner of the cosmos. "The earth," declares Farrar (1987, 16), "by occult theory and scientific fact" (i.e., Lovelock's musings) is a "living entity." The "frontiersmen of science" (i.e., Lovelock) are currently discovering the "coherence of that multi-leveled reality which occultism has always recognized." See Beardsley's essay for a delightful and trenchant presentation of the case.

5. Quotation marks indicate direct quotations from my tapes or from my notes. In many instances I do not cite explicitly the individual source of the verbalization, either because the context makes the source clear or because the significance of the passage does not require an explicit designation.

6. Miriam Simos's [Starhawk's] *The Spiral Dance* is among the most influential texts of modern Witchcraft. I make extensive use of it in the first part of Chapter 3, and I refer the reader to the bibliographical information at the end of the first part of Chapter 3.

Chapter 4. Bewitchment Everywhere

1. I urge the reader here to reexamine my comments on Chapter 4 made in this book's *Preface*.

2. Subsequent references to this work will appear in the text with the abbreviation *S* followed by a page number. The emphasis in this passage has been added by me.

3. Subsequent references to Einzig will appear in the text with the abbreviated form *PM* followed by page number.

4. Thomas Crump points out in his volume *The Phenomenon of Money* (London: Routledge Kegan Paul, 191, 17) that "one discovers the origin of specie in precious ornaments which are brought out for display in certain *rites de passage*—generally related to birth, marriage, and death."

5. I am working with a manuscript copy of this paper sent to me by its author.

6. Another excellent discussion of the degree to which the computer can become a psychological object for people is Sherry Turkle's *The Second Self* (New York: Simon and Schuster, 1984). Ms. Turkle writes on p. 17, "For adults and for children who play computer games, who use the computer for manipulating words, information, visual images, and especially for those who learn to program, computers enter into the development of personality, of identity, and even of sexuality."

References

Adler, M. 1986. *Drawing down the moon.* Boston: Beacon.

Ainsworth, M. 1983. Patters of infant-mother attachment. In *Human Development.* Ed. D. Magnusson and V. Allen. New York: Academic Press.

Arlow, J. 1984. Disturbances in the time sense. *Psychoanalytic Quarterly* 53:13–37.

Asbach, C., and V. Schermer. 1987. *Object relations, the self, and the group.* London: Routledge and Kegan Paul.

Bachelard, G. 1969. *The poetics of space.* Boston: Beacon.

Barrow, J., and F. Tipler. 1986. *The anthropic cosmological principle.* New York: Oxford University Press.

Basch, M. 1981. Psychoanalytic interpretation and cognitive transformation. *International Journal of Psychoanalysis* 62:151–74.

Beardsley, T. 1989. Gaia: An overview. *Scientific American.* December, pp. 35–36.

Becker, E. 1975. *Escape from evil.* New York: The Free Press.

Behrends, R., and S. Blatt. 1985. Internalization and psychological development throughout the life cycle. *The Psychoanalytic Study of the Child,* 40:11–39.

Berger, L. 1985. *Psychoanalytic theory and clinical relevance.* New York: Analytic Press.

Bergler, Edmund. 1959. *Money and emotional conflicts.* New York: International Universities Press.

Bettelheim, B. 1976. *The uses of enchantment: The meaning and importance of fairy tales.* New York: Alfred A. Knopf.

Bretanne, A. 1989. The sacred prostitute [Review]. *Shared Vision* (Vancouver, B.C.), 14:10.

Broughton, J. 1988. "Machine dreams: Computers in the fantasies of young adults." In *Individual, Society, and Communication.* Ed. R. Rieber. New York: Cambridge University Press.

Brown, N. O. 1959. *Life against death.* New York: Vintage.

Cabot, L. 1989. *Power of the witch.* New York: Delacorte Press.

Campbell, J. 1982. *Grammatical man: Information, entropy language, and life.* New York: Simon and Schuster.

Carrington, H., and S. Muldoon. 1929. *The projection of the astral body.* London: Rider.

Chodorow, N. 1978. *The reproduction of mothering.* Berkeley: University of California Press.

Churchland, P., and P. Churchland. 1990. Could a machine think? *Scientific American,* January 1990, pp. 32–37.

Collomb, H. 1978. Witchcraft-anthropophagia and dyadic relationship. *Psyche* 33:463–82.

Crowley, V. 1989. *Wicca: The old religion in the new age.* Wellingborough: Aquarian Press.

Crump, T. 1981. *The phenomenon of money.* London: Routledge Kegan Paul.

Cunningham, S. 1988. *The truth about witchcraft today.* St. Paul: Llewellyn Publications.———. 1989. *Wicca: A guide for the solitary practitioner.* St. Paul: Llewellyn Publications.

Delgado, J. 1971. *Physical control of the mind.* New York: Harper and Row.

de Mause, L. 1982. *Foundations of psychohistory.* New York: Creative Roots.

Desmonde, W. 1976. On the anal origin of money. In *The Psychoanalysis of Money.* Ed. E. Borneman. New York: Urizen Books, pp. 125–30.

Dorpat, T. 1988. Man and mind: Collected papers of Jeanne Lampel-De Groot. *Seattle Institute for Psychoanalysis Newsletter* 2: 4–5.

Dreyfus, H. 1972. *What computers can't do.* New York: Harper and Row.

Drury, N. 1985. *Dictionary of mysticism and the occult.* New York: Harper and Row.

Edelman, M. 1988. *Constructing the political spectacle.* Chicago: University of Chicago Press.

Eigen, M. 1985. Toward Bion's starting point. *International Journal of Psychoanalysis* 66: 321–30.

Eliade, M. 1976. Some observations on European witchcraft. In *Occultism, witchcraft, and cultural fashions.* Chicago: University of Chicago Press.

Elmer-Dewitt, P. 1988. Fast and smart. *Time,* 28 March 1988, pp. 40–44.

Erikson, E. 1987. *A way of looking at things: Selected papers 1930–1980.* New York: W. W. Norton.

Farrar, J. and S. 1984. *The witches' way.* Custer, Wash.: Phoenix Publishing Co.

———. 1987. *The witches' goddess.* Custer, Wash.: Phoenix Publishing Co.

Fjermedal, G. 1988. Brain trusts. *Omni,* June 1988, pp. 45–50, 78–79.

Frazer, J. 1890. *The golden bough.* London: Macmillan.

Freud, S. 1985. *The complete letters to Wilhelm Fliess.* Ed. J. M. Masson. Cambridge, Mass.: Harvard University Press.

Furnham, A., and A. Lewis. 1986. *The economic mind.* Brighton: Harvester Press.

Galbraith, J. 1972. *The new industrial state.* New York: Mentor Books.

Gardner, G. 1959. *The meaning of witchcraft.* New York: Magickal CHilde, Inc.

———. 1988. *Witchcraft today.* Lakemont, Georgia: Copple House Books.

Gesell, S. 1958. *The natural economic order.* London: Peter Owen.

Gilligan, C. 1982. *In a different voice.* Cambridge, Mass.: Harvard University Press.

Graves, R. 1946. *The white goddess.* London: Faber.

Graves, R. 1964. Witches in 1964. *Virginia Quarterly Review* 40:550–59.

Greenacre, P. 1971. The transitional object and the fetish. *Psychoanalytic Quarterly,* 40:384–85. Reported by Vivian Fromberg.

Grostein, J. 1978. Inner space: Its dimensions and coordinates. *International Journal of Psychoanalysis* 59:53–61.

Hartocollis, P. 1974. Origins of time. *Psychoanalytic Quarterly* 43:243–61.

Hendy, M. 1985. *Studies in the Byzantine monetary economy.* Cambridge, Eng.: Cambridge University Press.

Hubert, H., and M. Mauss. 1964. [1898]. *Sacrifice: Its nature and function.* Chicago: University of Chicago Press.

James, W. 1890. *Principles of psychology.* New York: Holt.

Japan-American Series. 1989. Narrated by Dick Cavett. KCTS, Channel 9, Seattle, Washington. 28 November 1989, 12:00 p.m.

Jastrow, R. 1978. Toward an intelligence beyond man's. *Time,* 20 February 1978, p. 47.

Johnson, R. 1990. Artificial intelligence. *Omni,* February 1990, p. 28.

Jones, R. 1982. *Physics as metaphor.* New York: Meridian Books.

Kleinberg, J. 1976. *How you can learn to live with computers.* Philadelphia: Lippincott.

Kluckhohn, C. 1982. Navaho witchcraft. In *Witchcraft and Sorcery,* 2d ed. Ed. M. Marwick. Harmondsworth: Penguin.

Koenigsberg, R. 1989. *Symbiosis and separation: Towards a psychology of culture.* New York: Library of Social Science.

Mahler, M., and M. Furer. 1968. *On human symbiosis and the vicissitudes of individuation.* New York: International Universities Press.

Mahler, M., Pine, F., and A. Bergman. 1975. *The psychological birth of the human infant.* New York: Basic Books.

Malinowski, B. 1925. [1982]. Sorcery as mimetic representation. In *Witchcraft and Sorcery,* 2d ed. Ed. M. Marwick. Harmondsworth: Penguin.

Neale, W. 1977. *Monies in society.* San Francisco: Chandler and Sharp.

Neubauer, P. 1985. Preoedipal objects and object primacy. *The Psychoanalytic Study of the Child* 40:163–82.

Neumann, E. 1970. *The great mother.* Princeton, N.J.: Princeton University Press.

Nietzsche, F. 1966. *Beyond good and evil.* New York: Vintage.

———. 1967. *The birth of tragedy.* New York: Vintage.

Person, E. 1989. *Dreams of love and fateful encounters.* London: Penguin.

Pines, D. 1980. Skin communication. *International Journal of Psychoanalysis* 61:315–24.

Posinsky, S. 1976. Yurok shell money and 'pains.' In *The Psychoanalysis of Money.* Ed. E. Borneman. New York: Urizen Books, pp. 188–95.

Reich, W. 1949. *Character analysis.* New York: Orgone Institute Press.

Rheingold, J. 1964. *The fear of being a woman.* New York: Grune and Stratton.

Rizzuto, A. 1979. *The birth of the living god.* Chicago: University of Chicago Press.

Roheim, G. 1955. *The origin and function of magic.* New York: International Universities Press.

———. 1969. *Psychoanalysis and anthropology.* New York: International Universities Press.

———. 1971. *The origin and function of culture.* New York: Doubleday.

———. 1976. Primal forms and the origin of property. In *The Psychoanalysis of Money.* Ed. E. Borneman. New York: Urizen Books, pp. 153–64.

Roland, A. 1988. *In search of self in India and Japan.* Princeton, N.J.: Princeton University Press.

Roustang, F. 1976. *Dire mastery: Discipleship from Freud to Lacan.* Baltimore, Md.: Johns Hopkins University Press.

Russell, J. 1980. *A history of witchcraft.* London: Thames and Hudson.

Sagan, E. 1985. *At the dawn of tyrrany.* New York: Knopf.

———. 1988. *Freud, women, and morality: The psychology of good and evil.* New York: Basic Books.

Schafer, R. 1968. *Aspects of internalization.* New York: International Universities Press.

Schrage, M. 1990. Artificial life in the process of evolution. *Los Angeles Times,* 8 February 1990, pp. D1, D19.

Searle, J. 1990. Is the brain's mind a computer program? *Scientific American,* January 1990, pp. 26–31.

Searles, J. 1984. Transference responses in borderline patients. *Psychiatry* 47:37–48.

Simos, M. [Starhawk] 1979. *The spiral dance.* New York: Harper and Row.

———. 1988. *Dreaming the dark.* Boston: Beacon Press.

Spitz, R. 1965. *The first year of life.* New York: International Universities Press.

Steffens, H. 1974. Science as a creative art. In *Science, Technology, and Culture.* Ed. H. Muller. New York: AMS Press.

Stein, H. 1981. *Psychoanalytic anthropology and psychohistory.* Presented to the Fourth Annual Convention of the International Psychohistorical Association, New York City, 11 June 1981.

———. 1984. Culture change, symbolic object loss, and restitutional process. *Psychoanalysis and Contemporary Thought,* 8:301–32.

Steinzor, B. 1979. Death and the construction of reality. *Omega: Journal of Death and dying* 9:97–124.

Stern, D. 1977. *The first relationship: Mother and infant.* Cambridge, Mass.: Harvard University Press.

Stoller, R. 1964. A contribution to the study of gender identity. *International Journal of Psychoanalysis* 45:220–226.

Trevor-Roper, H. R. 1970. The European witch-craze and social change. In *Witchcraft and sorcery,* 1st ed. Ed. M. Marwick. Harmondsworth: Penguin.

Valiente, D. 1989. *The rebirth of witchcraft.* London: Robert Hale.

Vygotsky, L. 1979. *Thought and language* [1934]. Cambridge, Mass.: MIT Press.

Warren-Clarke, L. 1987. *The way of the goddess.* Bridport: Prism Press.

Weber, M. 1958. *The Protestant ethic and the spirit of capitalism.* New York: Charles Scribner's Sons.

Williams, L. 1989. André-Marie Ampère. *Scientific American,* January 1989, pp. 90–97.

Winnicott, D. W. 1974. *Playing and reality.* London: Penguin.

Wiseman, T. 1974. *The money motive.* London: Hutchinson.

Index

189